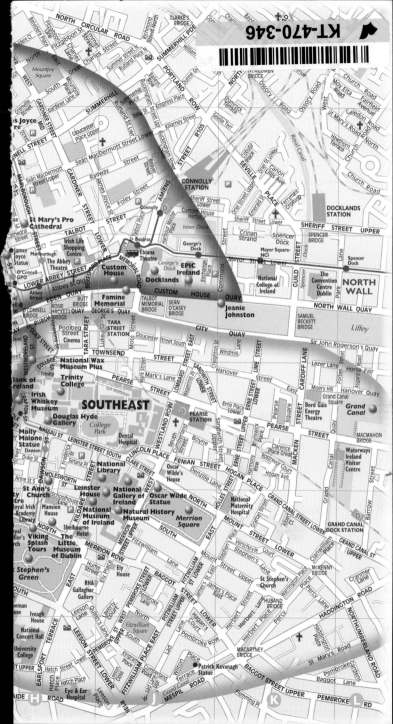

Items should be returned on or before the date shown below. Items not already requested by other borrowers may be renewed in person, in writing or by telephone. To renew, please quote the number on the barcode label. To renew online a PIN is required. This can be requested at your local library.
Renew online @ **www.dublincitypubliclibraries.ie**
Fines charged for overdue items will include postage incurred in recovery. Damage to or loss of items will be charged to the borrower.

Leabharlanna Poiblí Chathair Bhaile Átha Cliath
Dublin City Public Libraries

 Comhairle Cathrach
Bhaile Átha Cliath
Dublin City Council

Due Date	Due Date	Due Date

How to Use This Book

KEY TO SYMBOLS

➕ Map reference to the accompanying fold-out map

✉ Address

☎ Telephone number

🕐 Opening/closing times

🍴 Restaurant or café

🚉 Nearest rail station

Ⓜ Nearest subway (Metro) station

🚌 Nearest bus route

🛳 Nearest riverboat or ferry stop

♿ Facilities for visitors with disabilities

❓ Other practical information

▷ Further information

ℹ Tourist information

✋ Admission charges: Expensive (over €8), Moderate (€3–€8) and Inexpensive (€3 or less)

This guide is divided into four sections

● Essential Dublin: An introduction to the city and tips on making the most of your stay.

● Dublin by Area: We've broken the city into four areas, and recommended the best sights, shops, entertainment venues, nightlife and places to eat in each one. Suggested walks help you to explore on foot.

● Where to Stay: The best hotels, whether you're looking for luxury, budget or something in between.

● Need to Know: The info you need to make your trip run smoothly, including getting about by public transportation, weather tips, emergency phone numbers and useful websites.

Navigation In the Dublin by Area chapter, we've given each area of the city its own color, which is also used on the locator maps throughout the book and the map on the inside front cover.

Maps The fold-out map accompanying this book is a comprehensive street plan of Dublin. The grid on this fold-out map is the same as the grid on the locator maps within the book. We've given grid references within the book for each sight and listing.

Contents

Introducing Dublin

Building and renovation in Dublin continues at full speed, even long after the buoyant "Celtic Tiger" of the 1990s was tamed. The city is still buzzing, youthful and cosmopolitan, with history on show at every turn.

With the economic boom came an influx of artists, musicians, film-makers, chefs and designers attracted by tax concessions and inexpensive property. Ireland's success made it one of the most expensive countries in Europe. Then came the world recession. A downturn in the economy saw sky-high property values plummet and jobs disappear. The Luas tram system and the Port Tunnel are two legacies of the high-spending years that have made travel in and around Dublin much easier. The spectacular Samuel Beckett Bridge has given the city a new landmark, plus there are new bridges in the pipeline.

To the visitor, there are few signs of economic troubles. There's a buzz in the streets and the stylish restaurants and cafés, pubs and smart bars always seem busy. Shopping is as good as ever, and sales make the merchandise, from designer fashion to traditional and modern crafts, even more tempting. Dublin's cultural scene thrives, with theater productions, concerts and big stars performing at music venues, including the state-of-the-art 14,000-seater 3Arena. Traditional Irish music drifts from pubs, and DJs keep clubs hopping into the early hours.

If some building has stopped, much has continued. The innovative modern architecture of the rejuvenated Docklands has opened up exciting new urban spaces. But the old city is still there, its Georgian buildings and squares never ceasing to delight. Museums and art galleries are packed with well-displayed treasures, there's history at every turn, and the people are as welcoming as their legendary charm suggests. A visit to Dublin is a great experience.

FACTS AND FIGURES

THE SPIRE
● At 120m (394ft), the O'Connell Street sculpture is one of the world's tallest.
● Constructed from reflective stainless steel, the top 12m (39ft) are illuminated.
● Its official name is Monument of Light, although locals rarely call it that.
● Completed in 2003, the Spire replaces Nelson's Pillar which was blown up in 1966.

WHAT'S THE *CRAIC*?

When used in Ireland "What's the *craic*?" generally means, What's happening? What's the gossip? Even President Obama asked that to a hall filled with students to great applause. In fact, although most visitors consider it an authentic Irish word, it's actually derived from a Scottish or northern English word, crack—although the meaning is much the same.

NICKNAMES

It is a tradition in Dublin to have nicknames for the numerous statues and monuments dotted around the city.
For example, spot the following:
● Flue with the View
● Hags with the Bags
● Tart with the Cart
● Stiletto in the Ghetto
● Crank on the Bank
● Quare in the Square

FASHIONABLE DISTRICT

Dignitaries and celebrities often stay slightly outside central Dublin. The fashionable area of Ballsbridge and Lansdowne Road, to the southeast, is near the Aviva Stadium, hosting international rugby and football, the Royal Dublin Society's arena and the embassy belt with its excellent restaurants and classy hotels. Dublin is relatively compact, so it doesn't take long to reach these areas from the city.

A Short Stay in Dublin

DAY 1

Morning It wouldn't be a true trip to Ireland without acquainting yourself with the black stuff and an early start at the **Guinness Storehouse** (▷ 30–31) will help you beat the crowds. You can get a bus down to St. James's Gate and spend a couple of hours touring the displays.

Mid-morning Take your free glass of Guinness and maybe a coffee at the Gravity Bar at the top of the Storehouse and you will be rewarded with great views of the city. Catch a bus or walk back to view **Christ Church Cathedral** (▷ 25), and a trip around the adjoining **Dublinia** (▷ 28–29) will give you an excellent insight into the medieval life of the city.

Lunch Walk from the cathedral down Lord Edward Street into Dame Street. Just opposite **Dublin Castle** (▷ 26–27) you will find a quaint tea shop, the **Queen of Tarts** (▷ 44), where you can get an excellent light lunch. After lunch you may wish to visit the castle and the **Chester Beatty Library** (▷ 24), a rare collection of priceless books and Oriental art.

Afternoon Continue to the bottom of Dame Street, taking a left turn into Anglesea Street. Carry on until you come to the quay, and take a left and go first right over the **Ha'penny Bridge** for good views of the River Liffey. Over the river cross two roads and you will come to the **shopping hubs** (▷ 59) of Abbey Street and Henry Street. To the right you can follow through to O'Connell Street.

Dinner Return over the Ha'penny Bridge and go straight into **Temple Bar** (▷ 34) with its choice of cosmopolitan restaurants and bars.

Evening Soak up the atmosphere of Temple Bar or enjoy a quieter drink at **Palace Bar** (▷ 40).

DAY 2

Morning *The Book of Kells* in **Trinity College** (▷ 72–73) is one of the most visited sights in Dublin; the library opens at 9.30am. Try to take a walking tour of the college grounds, led by a student, afterward.

Mid-morning Walk to the front of the college and into Dublin's premier shopping street, Grafton Street, with its high street names and designer shops. Stop for a coffee at the famous **Bewley's Café** (▷ 84–85). At the bottom of Grafton Street you will come to the **St. Stephen's Green Centre** (▷ 80–81), with **St. Stephen's Green** (▷ 70–71) to the left.

Lunch If the weather is nice have a picnic in the park—where you might catch a concert in summer—or grab a bite to eat at the mall. Or take a short walk to Drury Street to enjoy lunch in one of its many restaurants.

Afternoon Take a stroll round the green, then take the exit to the north and cross over to Kildare Street. This is where you will find the grandest buildings in the city and fine museums, including the **National Museum** (▷ 68–69) with archeological treasures. Continue round to **Merrion Square** (▷ 75) with blue plaques on certain buildings noting former residents, then inside the tiny park, to spot the wonderful reclining statue of **Oscar Wilde** (▷ 76).

Dinner Merrion Square has many of Dublin's top restaurants. Treat yourself at **Restaurant Patrick Guilbaud** (▷ 88) in the **Merrion Hotel** (▷ 112), the Michelin-starred **L'Ecrivain** (▷ 85) or classic Italian in the **Unicorn** (▷ 88).

Evening You can choose here from traditional pubs like **Doheny and Nesbitt** or the classy **Horseshoe Bar** at the Shelbourne Hotel (▷ 82).

►►►

Chester Beatty Library
▷ **24** Its galleries show off a rich collection of Oriental and religious objects.

Christ Church Cathedral
▷ **25** This has been the seat of Irish bishops since the time of Viking Dublin.

Collins Barracks ▷ **40**
An impressive building houses the national decorative arts collection.

Trinity College ▷ **72–73**
Ireland's premier seat of learning is home to one of the world's most beautiful books.

Temple Bar ▷ **34** With its bohemian reputation and buzzing nightlife, you'll rarely get a quiet pint here.

St. Stephen's Green
▷ **70–71** Take a quiet break in this pleasant green space in the heart of Georgian Dublin.

St. Patrick's Cathedral
▷ **33** Visit the embodiment of history and heritage of the Irish people.

National Museum
▷ **68–69** See exhibits of Ireland's prehistoric and Viking treasures.

National Gallery ▷ **67**
Ireland's foremost collection of art pays homage to the old masters.

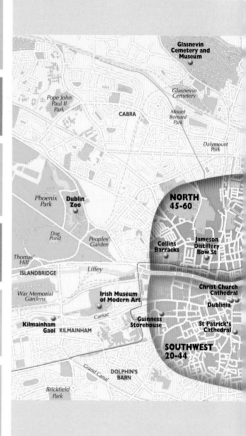

Marsh's Library ▷ **32**
An impressive collection is housed in Ireland's first public library.

The Little Museum of Dublin ▷ **66** A fascinating collection that documents 20th-century life in Dublin.

Kilmainham Gaol ▷ **96**
This infamous jail offers a profound insight into Irish history.

These pages are a quick guide to the Top 25, which are described in more detail later. Here they are listed alphabetically, and the tinted background shows the area they are in.

ESSENTIAL DUBLIN TOP 25

(Map showing Dublin with areas labelled: DRUMCONDRA, Griffith Park, MARINO, Royal Canal, PHIBSBOROUGH, Croke Park, GAA Museum, Tolka, Fairview Park, EAST WALL, Dublin Writers Museum, James Joyce Centre, Dublin City Gallery The Hugh Lane, GPO Witness History, EPIC Ireland, NORTH WALL, Liffey, Temple Bar, Dublin Castle, Chester Beatty Library, Marsh's Library, Trinity College, National Museum of Ireland, National Gallery of Ireland, The Little Museum of Dublin, St Stephen's Green, Iveagh Gardens, Fitzwilliam Square, Merrion Square, RINGSEND, Dodder, SOUTHEAST 61-88, RANELAGH, Grand Canal, BALLSBRIDGE)

Shopping

The delight of shopping in bustling Dublin lies in the compact nature of the city and the proximity of the best shopping areas to one another. Top local designers and major fashion brands are represented, as are traditional stores and retro shops.

Variety Is the Key

What really makes shopping in Dublin so rewarding is the variety of shops to be found there. Specialist shops tuck in alongside high street names, and home-grown talent blossoms amid international brands. Crafts-people merge the traditional with the modern while they continue to work in wood, silver, glass, ceramics, linen and wool—their designs stylishly up-to-the-minute. In Dublin you can find the best in beautifully made items, trendy home interiors and top-quality Irish food products.

Shopping Areas

Grafton Street, located south of the river, has always been considered the smart shopping area of the city. With its street musicians and colorful flower stalls, there's always a buzz in this pedestrian street lined with international and Irish fashion designer shops and chain stores, with the iconic Bewley's an essential coffee-stop along the way. Drury Street is seeing new independent boutiques, homeware stores and cafés popping up. Nearby, the Powerscourt Centre is the antidote to modern shopping malls. This fine 18th-century Georgian mansion is home to more than 40 specialty

KNOW YOUR *BODHRÁN* FROM YOUR BANJO

The *bodhrán* (pronounced "bough-rawn") is a simple and very old type of frame drum made of wood with animal skin—usually goat—stretched over the frame and decorated. It is played with a double-ended stick, rather than struck with the hands. Played for centuries in Ireland, it came onto the world stage in the 1960s with the rise of the Irish band The Chieftains. If you can't master the technique, try hanging it on your wall!

Brown's store (top); fashionable Grafton Street (middle); Crown Alley, Temple Bar (bottom)

boutiques as well as restaurants, bars and cafés. The Trinity College end of Grafton Street, Suffolk Street and Nassau Street are famed for their Irish design shops. The major department stores and big, bright and airy shopping centers are north of the river on O'Connell Street and Henry Street. With good parking, this revitalized area is popular with Dublin shoppers.

Irish Products

Sample bohemian South Great George's Street, filled with second-hand, retro and ethnic stores. Explore Temple Bar's cobbled winding streets for unusual finds and Saturday markets. Francis Street is Dublin's antiques quarter, home to wonderful Irish furniture and silverware. Shop for Aran knitwear—every sweater is unique— and Donegal tweed, Waterford, Tipperary and Galway crystal, Mosse pottery, Belleek porcelain, Orla Kiely bags and fine Irish linen. Jewelry has a special place in Dublin; look for the exquisite replicas of the Tara Brooch, Claddagh rings and Celtic knots mixing modern design with age-old tradition, and the work of new young designers with creative flair, especially around Cow's Lane and the outdoor Designer Mart (held there on Saturdays). In home interior shops you'll find contemporary designs based on time-honored patterns. Dublin is also the place to buy traditional musical instruments. And although much is mass-produced in Asia, kitsch is still part of Irish culture. Examples of leprechauns, shamrocks and shillelaghs can be found in profusion.

Merrion Square (top); CHQ Building, Docklands (middle); Powerscourt Townhouse (bottom)

LOCAL DELICACIES

Breads, farmhouse cheeses and salmon are a few of the local delights, along with handmade fresh cream chocolates and truffles. The Saturday market in Meeting House Square is a great place to buy these products. Look for Guinness-flavored toffees and Irish Porter cake. The Jameson Distillery sells all manner of Irish whiskey-flavored items—truffles, jams, fudge, chutney—but don't forget a bottle of the real thing.

Shopping by Theme

Whether you're looking for a department store, a quirky boutique, or something in between, you'll find it all in Dublin. On this page shops are listed by theme. For a more detailed write-up, see the individual listings in Dublin by Area.

Dublin by Night

Whether you like clubs, cocktail bars or traditional pubs, there is no shortage of venues. Dublin's theaters are famous. Big-name stars and hit musicals pack the massive 3Arena, and other venues feature a wide repertoire of plays and opera, or perhaps you prefer to catch one of the latest releases at the cinema.

Anyone for a Drink?

Dublin pubs are an institution and pub crawls make for a great night out, especially when you try to track down the thickest and tastiest pint of Guinness or Murphy's, or a lighter lager—Harp is brewed in Dublin. Although most pubs close at 11pm, 11.30pm or 12.30am, some pubs, bars and clubs serve alcohol late—until 2.30am on one or more nights. There is a smoking ban in all indoor venues. Watch out for leaflets detailing Irish music or jazz and rock sessions in many pubs and bars.

Laughter or Dancing?

Expanding fast, Dublin's comedy scene sees plenty of new talent emerging and comedy clubs seem to open all the time. There is stand-up comedy at many pubs every night; on open-mic nights comedians and other acts battle it out to be acclaimed as the night's best act. The Comedy Cellar at the International Bar on Wicklow Street hosts internationally renowned comedians and is famed for attracting rising stars. Clubs pulse with hard-core, garage, techno, electro, deep funk, house and chart toppers.

Cheers in Irish is sláinte. Have a traditional night out in a pub or go to one of Dublin's historic theaters

---

MERRION SQUARE

Evening light is kind to Dublin's Georgian architecture. Under illumination, the imposing buildings and elegant squares resemble the set of a magnificent period drama. Take an evening stroll around Merrion Square, down Merrion Street Upper and on to Baggot Street to see the dramatic sight of the illuminated National Museum and the Government Buildings.

Where to Eat

During Ireland's boom years, restaurants and bars opened up at a bewildering rate, many of them extremely good. Young, talented Irish chefs transformed the menus, placing great emphasis on local ingredients, and the number of Michelin stars grew. It's not all about top-class gourmet; there are plenty of atmospheric cafés, riverside restaurants and cozy bistros.

What's on Offer?

Look for good-value lunch specials and pre-theater menus, served before 7pm, when even upscale restaurants become affordable. While the choice of dishes may be smaller, there's no dip in quality. The vast array of restaurants reflects Dublin's cosmopolitan character, from Mediterranean and European cuisines through Thai, Japanese, Chinese and Malaysian to Middle Eastern specialties. Wherever you eat, portions are usually generous.

Irish Cooking

Many pubs still offer traditional fare but in restaurants and bistros, New Irish Cuisine has replaced the time-honored, rather heavy dishes. Innovative chefs are taking the country's fine, fresh ingredients and creating light, modern menus full of taste and stylishly presented.

Mealtimes

Breakfast may be served from 7am until 10am and lunch from 12 until 2.30pm, but with so many cafés, bistros and pubs open all day, finding something to suit is never a problem. Dinner is often served from around 5.30pm in restaurants and last orders could be at 10pm, but many ethnic restaurants keep later hours.

DRESS CODE

As with most things in life, the Irish take a very laid-back approach to dress codes. Casual attire is fine in all but the most expensive restaurants and some of the smarter hotel restaurants.

There is so much on offer in Dublin, from oyster bars and historic cafés to stylish and trendy eateries

Where to Eat by Cuisine

There are plenty of places to eat to suit all tastes and budgets in Dublin. On this page they are listed by cuisine. For a more detailed description of each restaurant, see Dublin by Area.

ESSENTIAL DUBLIN WHERE TO EAT BY CUISINE

Top Tips For...

These great suggestions will help you tailor your ideal visit to Dublin, no matter how you choose to spend your time. Each suggestion has a fuller write-up elsewhere in the book.

BEST IRISH BUYS

Brown Thomas department store (▷ 78) showcases established and up-and-coming Irish designers.
Avoca (▷ 78) store is full of all things Irish and the food hall is brimming with tasty delights.
Waltons (▷ 38) is the place for your musical instruments Irish-style, from *bodhráns* to whistles.

STYLE GURUS

Quirky and contemporary jewelry and home-wares can be bought at Cow's Lane Designer Studio (▷ 37), a short walk from Temple Bar.
From kitchen to living room you will be able to find something perfect for your home in Stock Design (▷ 81).

From traditonal to trendy—try some new styles while you are in Dublin and you won't be disappointed

EASTERN DELIGHTS

For an informal dining experience take a trip to the Mongolian Barbeque (▷ 43), and create your own dish from the ingredients provided.
Try a sophisticated Thai eating experience at Diep Le Shaker (▷ 85).
Head for the popular Japanese restaurant Yamamori (▷ 62) for noodles and sushi.

FISHY BUSINESS

For a real fishy treat head out to classy Cavistons in Dun Laoghaire (▷ 106).
DART out to Howth for the freshest of fish at the expensive, but worth it, King Sitric restaurant (▷ 106).
Down-to-earth fish and chips are at their best eaten straight out of the fryer from Leo Burdock's takeout (▷ 43).

Elegant, fashionable but always maintaining the traditional in Dublin's fair city

STAYING AT A GEORGIAN TOWN HOUSE

Four town houses in one, the Merrion (▷ 112) remains one of Dublin's most luxurious hotels—period elegance at its best.

Savor Georgian charm at the friendly Buswells hotel (▷ 110) in leafy Dublin 4.

Relax at Stauntons on the Green (▷ 111), a calm oasis with a garden in the heart of the city.

FASHIONABLE NIGHTLIFE

Dress to impress at the plush Lillie's Bordello (▷ 83) where the beautiful people hang out.

Opulence, big time, is on offer at the Café en Seine (▷ 82), a lively venue for cocktails and atmosphere.

TRADITIONAL MUSIC

Listen to Irish music every night at the Temple Bar pub The Merchants Arch (▷ 40).

For impromptu music visit O'Donoghue's (▷ 83), one-time haunt of the popular Irish band the Dubliners.

The Cobblestone (▷ 60), north of the river, has a regular program of Irish, blues and folk—check out the back room also.

The musical heritage of Ireland is alive and kicking in pubs all over the city

THINGS FOR KIDS

Dublin Zoo (▷ 92) provides plenty of cuddly and not so cuddly animals to view.

Start on the road and then take to the water on a Viking Splash tour (▷ 76).

Thrill and enthrall them at the National Wax Museum Plus (▷ 35).

Dublinia (▷ 28–29) is a must for exploring Viking Dublin.

AN INEXPENSIVE TRIP

There's something for everyone in Ireland's capital

Make the most of free admission to the National Museum (▷ 68) and National Gallery (▷ 67).
Cornucopia vegetarian restaurant (▷ 85) offers a wholesome breakfast.
Stroll through the parks or Georgian squares, such as Merrion Square (▷ 75)—it's free.

LUXURY

Be pampered at the Dawson Hotel (▷ 112), with its gorgeous Dawson Spa.
Dine at Ireland's leading French restaurant, Patrick Guilbaud (▷ 88).
Shop at Louise Kennedy (▷ 80) on Merrion Square for beautiful clothes and gifts.

THE GREAT OUTDOORS

Stroll in vast Phoenix Park (▷ 98) or the lesser-known peaceful Iveagh Gardens (▷ 75).
Take a trip on the DART (▷ 100–101) for great coast views and a breath of sea air.
Play a round of golf—the choice of courses is huge (▷ 105).

LITERARY GREATS

Find out about the city's famous scribes at the Dublin Writers Museum (▷ 50).
James Joyce is synonymous with Dublin—get an insight into the great man at the James Joyce Centre (▷ 53).
Oscar Wilde reclines languidly on a rock in Merrion Square, while his former home (▷ 76) is on the corner.
At the National Library (▷ 75), enjoy temporary exhibitions related to Ireland's writers.

Green space is abundant in Dublin's gorgeous Georgian squares

James Joyce statue, Earl Street

Dublin by Area

The Southwest

The southwest area is one of the most historically interesting districts of the city. From the early Celtic and Viking settlements, the medieval walled city of Dublin developed.

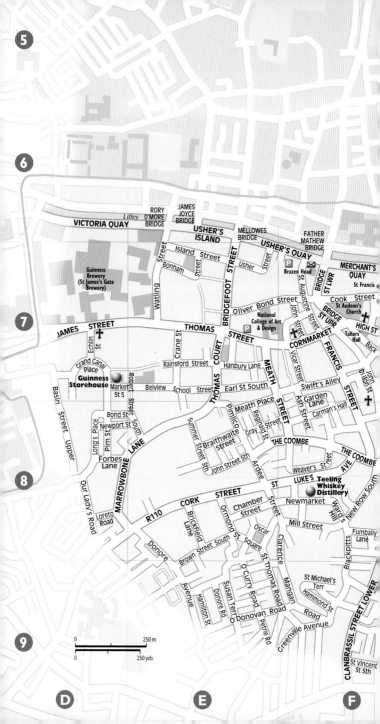

5

6

Liffey

RORY
O'MORE
BRIDGE

JAMES
JOYCE
BRIDGE

VICTORIA QUAY

USHER'S
ISLAND

MELLOWES
BRIDGE

USHER'S QUAY

FATHER
MATHEW
BRIDGE

Island   Street

Guinness
Brewery
(St James's Gate
Brewery)

Bonham

Street

Usher   Street

Street

Brazen Head

St Augustine Street

BRIDGE ST LWR

MERCHANT'S
QUAY

St Francis

Watling

BRIDGEFOOT STREET

Oliver   Bond   Street

Cook   Street

St Audoen's
Church

7

JAMES   STREET

THOMAS

National
College of Art
& Design

John   Street

BRIDGE ST UPR

HIGH ST

Echlin

St

STREET

THOMAS

STREET

CORNMARKET

Tailors'
Hall

Crane St

Rainsford   Street

Hanbury Lane

COURT

FRANCIS

Vicar Street

Back

John   Dillon   St

Grand Canal
Place

**Guinness
Storehouse**

Market
St S

Robert Street

Belview

School   Street

Earl St South

MEATH

Swift's Alley

STREET

Carman's Hall

Ash Street

STREET

8

Basin   Street   Upper

Long's Place

Bond St

Newport St

Pim St

MARROWBONE

LANE

Summer Street Sth

Pimlico

Braithwaite
Street

Reginald St

Gray St

Meath Place

Redmund St

THE COOMBE

Weaver's   Square

THE COOMBE

AVE

Forbes
Lane

Our Lady's Road

Loreto
Road

R110

John street Sth

Ardee

CORK

STREET

St

LUKE'S

**Teeling
Whiskey
Distillery**

Newmarket

New Row South

Ward's Hill

Brickfield
Lane

Chamber
Street

Street

Mill Street

Fumbally
Lane

Donore

Brown Street South

Ormond St South

Oscar
square

St Thomas Road

Clarence   Street

Blackpitts

CLANBRASSIL STREET LOWER

9

Avenue

Hamilton St

Donore Rd

Susan Terr

O'Curry Road

O'Donovan Road

Petrie Rd

Mangan

Road

St Michael's
Terr

Hammond St

Greenville Avenue

St Vincent
St Sth

0   250 m

0   250 yds

D

E

F

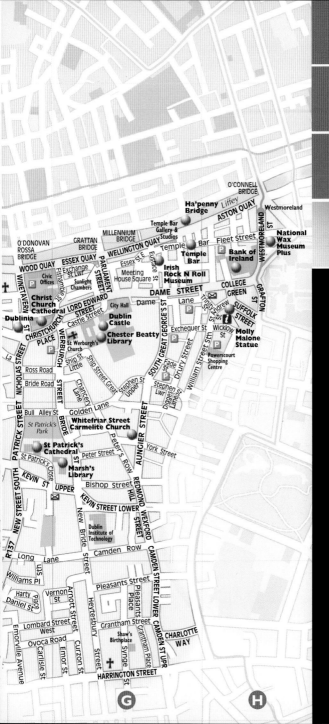

O'CONNELL BRIDGE

Westmoreland

Ha'penny Bridge

Liffey

ASTON QUAY

Temple Bar Gallery & Studios

Temple Bar

Fleet Street

National Wax Museum Plus

GRATTAN BRIDGE

MILLENNIUM BRIDGE

WELLINGTON QUAY

Temple Bar

O'DONOVAN ROSSA BRIDGE

ESSEX QUAY

Essex St

P

Bank of Ireland

WOOD QUAY

Exchange St Lwr

Essex St E

Eustace St

Fishamble St

PARLIAMENT STREET

Irish Rock N Roll Museum

Meeting House Square

Civic Offices

Sunlight Chambers

DAME STREET

COLLEGE GREEN

WINETAVERN ST

P

LORD EDWARD STREET

City Hall

Dame Lane

P

St Andrew St

SUFFOLK STREET

Christ Church Cathedral

Castle Street

Dublin Castle

GRAFTON ST

WESTMORELAND ST

Dublinia

CHRISTCHURCH PLACE

WERBURGH STREET

St Werburgh's Church

Chester Beatty Library

SOUTH GREAT GEORGES ST

Exchequer St

Fade St

Trinity St

Wicklow St

i

Molly Malone Statue

ST

La

Ship St Little

Ship Street Great

Drury Street

William Street S

Powerscourt Shopping Centre

Ross Road

NICHOLAS STREET

Bride Road

BRIDE STREET

Chancery Lane

Stephen St Upper

Stephen St Lwr

Digges Lane

Bull Alley St

St Patrick's Park

Golden Lane

AUNGIER STREET

Whitefriar Street Carmelite Church

York Street

PATRICK STREET

St Patrick's Cathedral

Peter Street

Peter's Row

St Patrick's Close

Marsh's Library

Bishop Street

KEVIN ST UPPER

KEVIN STREET LOWER

REDMOND'S HILL

WEXFORD STREET

NEW STREET SOUTH

New Bride Street

Dublin Institute of Technology

R137

Long Lane

Camden Row

CAMDEN STREET LOWER

CAMDEN ST UPR

Williams Pl

Harty Place

Vernon St

Arnott Street

Heytesbury Street

Pleasants Street

Pleasants Place

Grantham Place

CHARLOTTE WAY

Daniel St

Lombard Street West

Grantham Street

Shaw's Birthplace

Emorville Avenue

Ovoca Road

Curzon St

Emor St

Synge Street

Carlisle St

HARRINGTON STREET

G   H

Chester Beatty Library

Hidden away behind the ivy, the Chester Beatty Library reveals its Chinese ceiling

THE BASICS

cbl.ie

🔲 G7

✉ Dublin Castle

☎ 407 0750

🕐 Mon–Fri 10–5 (closed Mon Nov–Feb), Sat 11–5, Sun 1–5

🍴 Café

🚉 Tara Street

🚌 Cross-city buses

♿ Good

💷 Free

❓ Audio-visual presentations. Free guided tours. Roof Garden

HIGHLIGHTS

● New Testament papyri
● Qu'ran manuscripts
● Persian and Mughal paintings
● Jade snuff bottles

American-born Sir Alfred Chester Beatty is one of the few people to have been made an honorary citizen of Ireland, a gesture made in gratitude for the rare and priceless art collection that he bequeathed to the nation in 1956.

Hidden treasure The library and oriental art gallery named after its founder and benefactor, Sir Alfred Chester Beatty (1875–1968), is one of Dublin's jewels but is often overlooked. The unique collection is displayed on two floors in a converted Georgian building.

Masterpieces Alfred Chester Beatty, a successful mining engineer born in New York and knighted for his services to Britain as an advisor to Winston Churchill during World War II, devoted an important part of his life to the search for manuscripts and objets d'art of the highest quality. The collections range from c2700bc up to the present day, and stretch geographically from Japan to Europe. Religious writings range from one of the earliest known New Testament papyri to the Qu'rans, all masterpieces of calligraphy. There is a wealth of Persian and Mughal miniature paintings as well as wonders of the East such as Burmese and Siamese painted fairy-tale books or *parabaiks*, Chinese silk paintings and jade snuff bottles, and Japanese *netsuke* and woodblock prints. Permanent exhibitions are focused on two themes: Arts of the Book and Sacred Traditions. The library also stages temporary exhibitions.

Christ Church Cathedral

The superb nave (left); majestic Christ Church Cathedral (right)

Christ Church Cathedral is not only one of Dublin's oldest stone buildings but it is also perhaps the Normans' most outstanding contribution to Irish architecture. It reflects 1,000 years of worship in Ireland.

History The older of Dublin's two cathedrals, Christ Church was founded by the Norse king Sitric Silkenbeard in 1038. The northern side of the choir and the south transept are the oldest parts of the existing stone structure and have been dated to just before 1180. This indicates that work started on it shortly after the Normans took over the city, employing masons brought over from England. The early Gothic nave, dated c1226–36, also reflects English taste. Its vault collapsed in 1562, leaving the north wall with an outward lean of about 45cm (18in).

Restoration The whole building would now be a ruin but for the Dublin whiskey distiller Henry Roe, who paid for its reconstruction between 1871 and 1878. The work was carried out under the direction of the English architect George Edmund Street, who added flying buttresses to keep the whole edifice standing. Look for the effigy of a knight in armor near the entrance. It represents Strongbow, leader of the Anglo-Normans, who captured Dublin in 1170 and was buried in the cathedral in 1176. An unusual feature is the original crypt, extending the entire length of the cathedral and housing the Treasury. Exhibits include a video of the cathedral's history.

THE BASICS

christchurchdublin.ie

✚ F7

✉ Christchurch Place

☎ 677 8099

🕐 Apr–Sep Mon–Sat 9.30–7, Sun 12.30–2.30, 4.30–7; Mar and Oct Mon–Sat 9.30–6, Sun 12.30–2.30, 4.30–6; Nov–Feb Mon–Sat 9.30–5, Sun 12.30–2.30

🚌 49A, 50, 51B, 54A, 65, 77, 123

♿ Good

💷 Moderate

HIGHLIGHTS

● 12th-century south transept
● Leaning north wall
● Knight's effigy
● Crypt and "Treasures of Christ Church"

Dublin Castle

- Powder Tower
- State Apartments
- Chapel Room

How many buildings in Europe can claim to have been the hub of a country's secular power for longer than Dublin Castle, the headquarters of English rule in Ireland for more than 700 years?

Ancient site Dublin Castle, now used for State occasions and presidential inaugurations, stands on the site of a much older Viking settlement. It occupies the southeastern corner of the Norman walled town overlooking the long-vanished black pool or *dubh linn* that gave the city its ancient Irish name. The excavated remains of one of its circular bastions, the Powder Tower, is shown on the guided tour.

Interior After a fire in 1684, the interior was almost entirely rebuilt in the 18th and early

Clockwise from far left: Stone exterior of the Chapel Royale; the castle's atmospheric red drawing room; a fountain in the castle grounds; the impressive throne room; Courtyard at Castle Hall

19th centuries. On the south side of Upper Castle Yard are the lavish State Apartments, where the English king's viceroy lived until the castle was handed over to the Irish State in 1922. These regal rooms form the second half of the guided tour, which starts in the Powder Tower. The Gothic Chapel Royal is famed for its carved stone heads, carved oak galleries and stained-glass windows. Unfortunately, as this is a government building, some areas of the castle are occassionally closed because of official functions.

City Hall Right next door to the castle is the imposing City Hall with its multimedia exhibition, "The Story of the Capital" (Mon–Sat 10–5.15). Check out the fabulous domed ceiling in the entrance hall, with gilded paintwork.

THE BASICS

dublincastle.ie

➕ G7

✉ Dame Street

☎ 677 7129

🕐 Mon–Sat 9.45–4.45, Sun and public hols 10.45–4.45. State Apartments closed occasionally for functions

🍴 Restaurant/café

🚇 Tara Street

🚌 Cross-city buses

♿ State Apartments: good. Powder Tower: none

💷 Moderate

❓ Gardens, open Mon–Fri, not part of tour

Dublinia

● Re-creation of medieval Dublin
● Archeology
● Interactive re-created Medieval Fair
● Viking re-creations
● View over Dublin

If you want to know what made Dublin's Viking and medieval ancestors tick, visit Dublinia, with its Viking exhibitions, and audio-visual and interactive displays.

Vivid re-creation Dublinia, as the town was first recorded on a map of c1540, is a vibrant re-creation of medieval Dublin life housed in the former Synod Hall. After the Vikings had re-established the city in this area during the 10th century, Hiberno-Norsemen and Normans occupied it from 1170 until the end of the Middle Ages—the time-span covered by Dublinia. In the section on Viking Dublin, kids can try on Viking clothes, try to decipher the runic alphabet and visit a cramped, smoky Viking house to get a feeling of the lifestyle and conditions.

Clockwise from far left: Vikings in traditional headgear; learn about life in medieval Dublin and meet the Vikings—but mind the stocks; the medieval village from above

Excavations More than 30 years of extensive excavations in the Dublinia area have uncovered many objects such as leatherwork, pottery (some fragments intricately decorated with amusing faces), floor tiles, jewelry and ships' timbers, which are also on view in the exhibition. An interesting audio-visual presentation of the city's history complements the series of life-size model tableaux that illustrate episodes from the past. "History Hunters" is an exciting exhibition that uncovers the world of archeology. There are artifacts including the locally found skeletal remains of a Viking warrior and a medieval woman. To complete your visit, climb the 96 steps in the tower of 15th-century St. Michael's Church, incorporated into the Synod Hall when it was constructed, for views of the city and river.

THE BASICS

dublinia.ie

➕ F7

✉ St. Michael's Hill, Christchurch

☎ 679 4611

🕐 Mar–Sep daily 10–6.30 (last admission 5.30); Oct–Feb daily 10–5.30 (last admission 4.30)

🚌 50, 51B, 78A

🍴 Café

♿ Dublinia: good. Tower and bridge: none

✋ Moderate

❓ Prebookable tours. Wheelchair accessible

Guinness Storehouse

HIGHLIGHTS

● Glass pint structure
● Brewing exhibition
● Transportation section
● Classic advertisements and memorabilia
● Rooftop view

TIPS

● The admission fee includes a complimentary pint of Guinness.
● Check out the flagship shop selling a range of Guinness merchandise.

Think Dublin, think Guinness. For more than 250 years, the black stuff has been an integral part of the city's economy and history. The Guinness Storehouse celebrates that legacy.

What's in a glass? The massive steel beams and pint-glass shaped, light-filled Atrium are a perfect introduction to this 1904 building. Within this glass structure your journey through the production process of a pint of Guinness begins. Simple, dramatic displays show the four basic ingredients—hops, barley, yeast and water—all of which you can touch, feel and smell. The displays provoke the senses as indicated on the huge wall label reading "Smells are delectable too, the heavy sleepy scent of hops—steam, hot metal, sweat."

Clockwise from far left: The cobblestone road in front of the old buildings remains from the early 1900s; the superb 21st-century atrium; each area of the Storehouse is visually striking as well as informative

Mine's a pint You follow the pint as it makes its way through the brewery of the past, founded by Arthur Guinness in 1759—a past still much in evidence today. Old machinery is cleverly used, doubling up as interactives to give you more information. From the brewing process you go to the transportation section, to view large-scale models. The advertising display is great fun, with popular memorabilia and a hall of fame recalling classic Guinness adverts. You learn how the brew has affected many aspects of Irish life as a supporter of the arts, festivals and sport, then finish your journey at the top of the glass, in the Gravity Bar, with a splendid view over Dublin and your free pint. Every year more than a million people visit the Storehouse, making it (for the past few years) Ireland's most popular visitor attraction.

THE BASICS

guinness-storehouse.com

✚ D7

✉ St. James's Gate

☎ 408 4800

🕐 Jul–Aug daily 9–8 (last admission 6pm); rest of year 9.30–7

🍴 Brewery Dining Hall, Gravity Bar, Arthur's Bar

🚌 51B, 78A from Aston Quay; 123 from O'Connell Street; Luas St. James's

♿ Excellent

💷 Expensive

❓ Shop

Marsh's Library

TOP 25

The oldest public library in Ireland is light years away from modern Dublin

THE BASICS

marshlibrary.ie

🕂 G8

✉ St. Patrick's Close

☎ 454 3511

🕐 Mon, Wed–Fri 9.30–5, Sat 10–5

🚌 Cross-city buses

♿ Few

💷 Inexpensive

HIGHLIGHTS

● Old-world atmosphere
● Oak bookcases
● "Cages" for rare works
● Books and manuscripts

This fine example of an 18th-century scholar's library has changed little since it opened more than 300 years ago. One of the few buildings in the city to retain its original purpose, it remains a calm oasis of scholarly learning.

Rare legacy In 1701, Archbishop Narcissus Marsh (1638–1713) built Ireland's first public library close to St. Patrick's Cathedral and filled it with his own books. In 1705 he acquired 10,000 more, purchased from the Bishop of Worcester. Two years later, the library was given official legal standing when the Irish parliament passed an Act for "settling and preserving a public library." The building is one of the city's rare legacies from the reign of Queen Anne and was designed by Sir William Robinson, responsible for the Royal Hospital at Kilmainham (▷ 95), using distinctive gray Dublin limestone on one side and red brick on the front.

Precious books Inside, the long gallery is flanked on each side by dark oak bookcases topped by carvings of an archbishop's miter. At the end of the L-shaped gallery are three alcoves, or "cages," where readers were locked in with the library's precious books. As an extra safeguard, chains were attached to the books (though not to the readers). Some 25,000 volumes fill the shelves. In a wide range of subjects and languages, they span the 15th to the early 18th centuries. The library also possesses some 300 manuscripts.

St. Patrick's Cathedral

St. Patrick's Cathedral
(left); the intricately
carved Knights of
St. Patrick choirstalls
(right)

"Here is laid the body of Jonathan Swift, Doctor of Divinity, Dean of this Cathedral Church, where fierce indignation can no longer rend the heart. Go traveller, and imitate, if you can, this earnest and dedicated champion of liberty."

Literary connections Jonathan Swift's epitaph is a fitting tribute to the personality most often associated with St. Patrick's Cathedral. The author of *Gulliver's Travels*, Swift was the cathedral's outspoken Dean from 1713 until his death in 1745. He and his beloved friend, Stella, are buried in the south aisle.

History Founded in 1191 near a sacred well where St. Patrick is said to have baptized pagans, Ireland's national cathedral was built in Early English Gothic style and completed by 1284. Like Christ Church (▷ 25), St. Patrick's was heavily restored in the 19th century, with funds from the Guinness family. The cathedral embodies the heritage of the Irish people and receives over 300,000 visitors every year.

Monuments Look for the tomb and effigy of the 17th-century adventurer Richard Boyle, Earl of Cork, and a memorial to the Irish bard and harpist Turlough O'Carolan (1670–1738). In the south choir aisle are two of Ireland's rare 16th-century monumental brasses. George Frederick Handel practiced on the cathedral's organ before the first public performance of his *Messiah* in 1742.

THE BASICS

stpatrickscathedral.ie

➕ F8

✉ St. Patrick's Close

☎ 453 9472

🕐 Mar–Oct Mon–Fri 9.30–5, Sat 9–6, Sun 9–10.30, 12.30–2.30, 4.30–6; Nov–Feb Mon–Sat 9.30–5, Sun 9–10.30, 12.30–4.30. Visiting restricted during services

🚌 Cross-city buses

♿ Good

👆 Moderate

❓ Living Stones exhibition explores St. Patrick's history. Guided tour (free) Mon–Sat 11.30, 2.30

HIGHLIGHTS

- Swift's bust and epitaph
- Medieval brasses
- Memorial to O'Carolan
- Organ
- Living Stones exhibition

Temple Bar

Traditional music at Oliver St. John Gogarty (left); advertising the black stuff (right)

THE BASICS

templebar.ie
➕ G7
Meeting House Square
➕ G7
✉ Temple Bar
🚆 Tara Street
🚌 Cross-city buses

HIGHLIGHTS

● Meeting House Square
● Pubs, bars and cafés
● Markets: food (every Sat 10–4.30, ▷ 38) in Meeting House Square; books (Sat, Sun 11–6) in Temple Bar Square
● Street theater

The area known as Temple Bar lies between Dame Street and the River Liffey. It takes its name from the Anglo-Irish aristocrat Sir William Temple, who owned land here in the 17th century. In Viking times it was the heart of the city.

Early beginnings Business flourished in Temple Bar from the early 17th century but the area fell into decline in the early 20th century and by the late 1980s had been proposed as the site for a new bus terminal. Objections were vociferous and the city's "left bank" began to take off.

Dublin's Cultural Quarter Today, pedestrian-friendly and with restricted vehicle access, this is a vibrant cultural district and the main draw for tourists with its mix of restaurants, shops, markets, pubs and bars. It is the venue for artists' studios, galleries, theater and music. Temple Bar's popularity has meant that at times there has been unwanted unruly behavior. It does still get rowdy at weekends, but during the day and on weekday nights it is great fun to be in. Nearby Cow's Lane, Dublin's oldest district, is the setting for Designer Mart, featuring innovative designers, held every Saturday.

Meeting House Square This square is the focus for performance art, the summer open-air cinema and the wonderful Saturday market (▷ 38, panel) which is a showcase of Irish artisan food suppliers and cooked delicacies.

More to See

BANK OF IRELAND
This imposing and curved Palladian building, whose foundations were laid in 1729, was the focus of Ireland's years of freedom in the late 18th century, originally as the upper and lower house of the old Irish Parliament.
✚ H7 ✉ 2 College Green ☎ 661 5933 ⏰ House of Lords: Mon–Fri 10–3.30 🚉 Tara Street 🚌 Cross-city buses ♿ Few 💷 Free ❓ Tours of House of Lords Tue 10.30, 11.30, 12.30

HA'PENNY BRIDGE
One of Dublin's most iconic landmarks, this was Ireland's first cast-iron bridge when it opened in 1816. The city's oldest pedestrian bridge, it was so named for the halfpenny toll once charged to pedestrians to cross—each way.
✚ G6 ✉ Wellington Quay to Bachelors Walk 🚌 Cross-city buses 💷 Free

IRISH ROCK N ROLL MUSEUM
irishrocknrollmuseum.com
Experience Irish music history of the last 30 years with this behind-the-scenes tour of a real-life rehearsal and recording studio. You can even record your own song. Outside, don't miss the striking Wall of Fame.
✚ G7 ✉ Curved Street, Temple Bar ☎ 635 1993 ⏰ Daily 11.30–5.30 🚌 Cross-city buses 💷 Expensive

MOLLY MALONE STATUE
This life-size bronze statue of Molly Malone with her wheelbarrow honors the fishmonger, of whom the famous song was written about. She is believed to have lived and worked in Dublin until her death in 1734. The statue was presented to the city in 1984, and was located on Lower Grafton Street, then moved to her new home, outside St. Andrew's Church, in 2014.
✚ H7 ✉ Suffolk Street 🚉 Pearse 🚌 Cross-city buses

NATIONAL WAX MUSEUM PLUS
waxmuseumplus.ie
Here, step through Irish history and a scary Chamber of Horrors; see lifelike wax models of Irish actors, musicians and sporting legends; and even make your own film to upload online. There's also a science zone with interactive exhibits.
✚ H6 ✉ Westmoreland Street ☎ 671 8373 ⏰ Daily 10–7 🚉 Tara Street 🚌 Cross-city buses 💷 Expensive

TEELING WHISKEY DISTILLERY
teelingdistillery.com
This is Dublin's first new whiskey distillery for more than 125 years. Tours explain the history of whiskey in Ireland, show the distilling process and end with a tasting session in the bar.
✚ F8 ✉ 13–17 Newmarket ☎ 531 0888 ⏰ 10–5.30 🚌 27, 56A, 77, 151 💷 Expensive ❓ Tours

WHITEFRIAR STREET CARMELITE CHURCH
whitefriarstreetchurch.ie
Full of shrines, Whitefriar's contains the relics of St. Valentine. The altar holds the medieval carved oak Madonna and Child, known as "Our Lady of Dublin."
✚ G8 ✉ 56 Aungier Street ☎ 475 8821 ⏰ Mon–Fri 7.30–6, Sat 7.30–7, Sun 7.30am–8pm. Mass daily 🚉 Pearse 🚌 Cross-city buses ♿ Good 💷 Free

THE SOUTHWEST MORE TO SEE

35

Walk Along the Quays

The English-born architect James Gandon (1743–1823) played an important role in the beautification of Dublin.

DISTANCE: 1.5km (1 mile) **ALLOW:** 45 minutes

START

GEORGE'S QUAY
➕ J6 🚌 Cross-city buses

END

FOUR COURTS (▷ 57)
➕ F6 🚌 Cross-city buses

❶ Start at George's Quay and look across to the Custom House (▷ 56), a magnificent neoclassical building, built by James Gandon between 1781 and 1791.

❽ Here you will have the best view, over the river, of the Four Courts (▷ 57), Gandon's second master-piece, built between 1786 and 1802.

❷ At O'Connell Bridge, glance left along Westmoreland Street to see the portico (c1784–89) that Gandon added to the Old Parliament House, now the Bank of Ireland (▷ 35).

❼ Continue past the Civic Offices on your left, where excavations unearthed a Viking site in the 1970s, until you reach Merchant's Quay. This was the site of the first Viking crossing of the River Liffey when they arrived in Dublin back in the ninth century.

❸ Continue upstream past the metal bridge, known as the Ha'penny Bridge, constructed in 1816. Carry on past the pedestrian Millennium Bridge.

❻ While still by the Grattan Bridge have a look at the striking sea horse statues. Just beyond is Betty Maguire's Viking Boat sculpture (20th century) outside the Civic Offices.

❹ At the Grattan Bridge look south along Parliament Street to Thomas Cooley's imposing City Hall (▷ 27), the headquarters of Dublin Corporation since 1852.

❺ City Hall was built in 1769, some time before Gandon arrived in Dublin.

ARTICLE

articledublin.com

Located in Lord Powerscourt's former dressing room, this luxury homeware store sells tableware, fabrics, stationery and more. Items include pieces from top Irish designers.

H7 ⊠ Powerscourt Centre, 59 South William Street ☎ 679 9268 ⊠ Pearse ⊟ Cross-city buses

CLADDAGH RECORDS

claddaghrecords.com

This specialist music shop is in a Temple Bar backstreet. It sells CDs and DVDs, from the countrified sound of Irish dance bands to the traditional and contemporary. The staff know their stuff.

G7 ⊠ 2 Cecilia Street, Temple Lane ☎ 677 0262 ⊠ Tara Street ⊟ Cross-city buses

COCOA ATELIER

Sample melt-in-the-mouth macaroons and exquisite handmade chocolates made on site, along with a super-rich cup of hot chocolate in this little store. Check out the overhead light fittings.

G7 ⊠ 30 Drury Street ☎ 675 3616 ⊟ Cross-city buses

COW'S LANE DESIGNER STUDIO

cowslanedesignerstudio.ie

Buy fashion, knits, jewelry and homewares from this design collective. On Saturdays, visit the outdoor Designer Mart in Cow's Lane.

G7 ⊠ Essex Street West, Temple Bar ☎ 524 0001 ⊠ Tara Street ⊟ Cross-city buses

DESIGN CENTRE

designcentre.ie

A boutique collection inside the Powerscourt Centre (▷ 38), this has fashion from renowned Irish and international designers. Look out for sophisticated accessories from designer Philip Treacy.

H7 ⊠ Powerscourt Centre, 59 South William Street ☎ 679 5718 ⊠ Pearse ⊟ Cross-city buses

EAGER BEAVER

Buy vintage clothes and accessories here for men and women, ranging from denim jackets to party dresses.

G7 ⊠ 17 Crown Alley, Temple Bar ☎ 677 3342 ⊠ Tara Street ⊟ Cross-city buses

FALLON & BYRNE

fallonandbyrne.com

Foodies make a beeline for this huge food hall, with deli counters, cheeses, charcuterie and breads—this is a 5-star supermarket. There's a small coffee bar also for fresh brews and cakes, and the Wine Cellar downstairs (▷ 41).

G7 ⊠ 11–17 Exchequer Street ☎ 472 1010 ⊟ Cross-city buses

FLIP

This shop is a favorite for Irish shoppers on the trail of vintage second-hand clothing from Europe and America. They have their own label, too.

G7 ⊠ 4 Fownes Street Upper, Temple Bar ☎ 671 4299 ⊠ Tara Street ⊟ Cross-city buses

GEORGE'S STREET ARCADE

georgesstreetarcade.ie

This covered, Victorian arcade, Ireland's oldest, has an eclectic array of shops and stalls. You'll find everything from vintage clothes at Retro and second-hand vinyl at Spindizzy Records to tempting gourmet food at Lolly & Cooks.

G7 ⊠ Between South Great George's Street and Drury Street ⊠ Pearse ⊟ Cross-city buses

THE HARLEQUIN

This store is loved for its classy vintage clothing and accessories, especially those from the 1920s. Check out the vintage handbags, which are a house specialty.

➕ G7 ✉ 13 Castle Market ☎ 671 0202
🚉 Pearse 🚌 Cross-city buses

INDUSTRY & CO

industryandco.com

It's hardly a conventional gift shop, but many of the items sold here make perfect presents: Irish and international designs, with everything from home ware to eco-leather bags.

➕ G7 ✉ 41 Drury Street ☎ 613 9111
🚌 Cross-city buses

JOHN FARRINGTON ANTIQUES

johnfarringtonantiques.com

This small shop specializes in antique jewelry, with a fabulous selection of one-off commissioned pieces using antique precious gems. Choose rings, bracelets, necklaces and even tiaras.

➕ G7 ✉ 32 Drury Street ☎ 679 1899
🚉 Pearse 🚌 Cross-city buses

MCCULLOUGH PIGOTT

mcculloughpigott.com

Highly respected by music lovers who while away the time gazing at the traditional Irish musical instruments and browsing through sheet music.

➕ G7 ✉ 11 William Street ☎ 677 3138
🚉 Pearse 🚌 Cross-city buses

O'SULLIVAN ANTIQUES

osullivanantiques.com

This is an Aladdin's cave of exquisite items from years gone by. Mahogany furniture, gilt mirrors, mantelpieces, garden statues and delicate glassware.

➕ F7 ✉ 43–44 Francis Street ☎ 454 1143
🚌 78A, 123

PEEKABOO

peekaboodesignstudios.com

For the dress for that special occasion, this shop creates made-to-order beautiful garments in gorgeous materials. You can also have your old dresses refurbished here.

➕ G7 ✉ 18 Lower Liffey Street ☎ 085 283 5232 (mobile) 🚉 Ormond Quay 🚌 Cross-city buses

POWERSCOURT CENTRE

powerscourtcentre.ie

A warren of boutiques, gift and craft stores, restaurants, cafés and art galleries in a Georgian town house. The Design Centre (▷ 37) is well worth a look.

➕ H7 ✉ 59 South William Street ☎ 679 4144 🚉 Pearse 🚌 Cross-city buses

WALTONS

waltons.ie

Waltons is a store for musicians, from wannabe rock stars to the stalwarts of the traditional scene, and has been an Irish music specialist since the 1920s. From *bodhráns* to whistles, pipes to accordions, plus sheet music, Irish songbooks and accessories.

➕ G7 ✉ 69–70 South Great George's Street ☎ 475 0661 🚉 Pearse 🚌 Cross-city buses

SATURDAY MARKET

Temple Bar's lively weekly food market in Meeting House Square (Sat 10–4.30) sells a variety of produce ranging from Japanese sushi to Mexican burritos. Local Irish produce includes fresh breads, jams, yogurts and vegetables. Those with a sweeter tooth will enjoy the handmade fudge and chocolate stalls or freshly cooked waffles and crêpes. Also cheeses, olives, oysters and more. It's a great place to head to at the start of the weekend.

Entertainment and Nightlife

THE ARK

ark.ie

This specially created cultural venue for children of all ages offers around 10 delightful art and culture events each year. There are regular plays and music workshops.

➕ G7 ✉ 11a Eustace Street ☎ 670 7788 🚋 Tara Street 🚌 Cross-city buses ℹ Check before visit; many events for school groups only

THE BAR WITH NO NAME

nonamebardublin.com

It may have no official name, but it has bags of personality inside, with a bunch of small bohemian living rooms with sofas, eclectic artwork, open fires and a huge heated terrace. It attracts arty locals, especially for weekend brunch.

➕ G7 ✉ 3 Fade Street ☎ 087 122 1064 (mobile) 🚌 Cross-city buses

BRAZEN HEAD

brazenhead.com

Reputedly the oldest bar in town—it has been trading since 1198—the Brazen Head has an old-world charm. It offers good food and drink and nightly Irish music sessions.

➕ F7 ✉ 20 Bridge Street Lower ☎ 679 5186 🚌 121

BUTTON FACTORY

buttonfactory.ie

In the Temple Bar Music Centre, this premier music venue holds themed club nights and live music.

➕ G7 ✉ Curved Street, Temple Bar ☎ 670 9105 🚋 Tara Street 🚌 Cross-city buses

HOGAN'S

This lively bar is popular with Dublin's clubbing crowd.

➕ G7 ✉ 35 South Great George's Street ☎ 677 5904 🚌 Cross-city buses

THE GEORGE

thegeorge.ie

Considered Dublin's first GLBT bar, this place still draws a mix of crowds. The low-lit front bar is good for a quiet drink, with its contrasting main club venue a lively space for regular events and theme nights. Look out for karaoke, drag acts and bingo nights.

➕ G7 ✉ South Great George's Street ☎ 671 3298 🚌 Cross-city buses

IRISH FILM INSTITUTE

ifi.ie

An art-house cinema showing independent Irish and international films, the IFI has occasional free events and curated seasons. It also has an informal bar/restaurant, plus a shop.

➕ G7 ✉ 6 Eustace Street, Temple Bar ☎ 679 5744 🚋 Tara Street 🚌 Cross-city buses

THE LONG HALL

Time seems to have stood still in this traditional hostelry, with a long bar, smoked glass and ornate paintwork.

➕ G7 ✉ 51 South Great George's Street ☎ 475 1590 🚌 Cross-city buses

THE MARKET BAR

marketbar.ie

Tucked away at the back of George's Street Arcade (▷ 37), this spacious bar is named after the meat market that stood here. High ceilings, a tapas menu

and a very cool vibe—with no music—make it a grown-ups' place for a drink.
🔹 G7 ✉ 14a Fade Street ☎ 613 9094
🚌 Cross-city buses

THE MERCHANTS ARCH

merchantsarch.ie

Enjoy traditional live music from several bands every night at this well regarded bar, plus there's food served all day. Big screens show Ireland's live sports events.
🔹 G7 ✉ 48–49 Wellington Quay ☎ 607 4010 🚌 Cross-city buses

THE NEW THEATRE

thenewtheatre.com

Accessed through the Connolly Bookshop, this intimate 66-seat venue showcases new Irish work.
🔹 G7 ✉ 43 East Essex Street, Temple Bar
☎ 670 3361 🚉 Tara Street 🚌 Cross-city buses

OLYMPIA

olympia.ie

Dublin's oldest theater, most recently refurbished in 2016, attracts singers, musicians, stage shows, comedy and pantomimes onto its ornate stage.
🔹 G7 ✉ 72 Dame Street ☎ 679 3323
🚉 Tara Street 🚌 Cross-city buses

PALACE BAR

thepalacebardublin.com

Established in 1843, this traditional pub still retains its old frosted glass and mahogany interior and was once a haunt of many literary giants of Dublin.
🔹 H6 ✉ 21 Fleet Street ☎ 671 7388
🚌 Cross-city buses

THE PORTERHOUSE

porterhousebrewco.com

Dublin's first microbrewery is still doing an excellent job. It brews ales, stouts,

three lagers and the occasional special on the premises, and stocks a huge range of bottled beers. Good food is served, and there's live music nightly.
🔹 G7 ✉ 16–18 Parliament Street, Temple Bar
☎ 679 8847 🚌 Cross-city buses

PROJECT ARTS CENTRE

projectartscentre.ie

From visual arts to dance, music and theater, in two performance spaces and a gallery, this contemporary arts space gives a chance for Irish talent to shine.
🔹 G7 ✉ 39 East Essex Street ☎ 881 9613
🚉 Tara Street 🚌 Cross-city buses

RÍ RÁ

theglobe.ie

Downstairs from the late-night Globe bar, DJs at this nightclub play a range of music, especially indie and electro.
🔹 G7 ✉ Dame Court ☎ 671 1220
🚉 Tara Street 🚌 Cross-city buses

SMOCK ALLEY THEATRE

smockalley.com

Dublin's first Theatre Royal opened on this site in 1662 and closed in 1787. The building was later converted into a church but reopened as a theater in

2012 after extensive renovation. It now stages contemporary drama and is home to the Gaiety School of Acting.
🔼 G7 ✉ 6–7 Exchange Street Lower ☎ 677 0014 🚆 Pearse 🚌 Cross-city buses ❓ Tours

STAG'S HEAD
thestagshead.ie
Built in 1770 and restyled in 1895, this pub has wonderful stained-glass windows, wood carvings and ironwork. Live music and good food.
🔼 G7 ✉ 1 Dame Court ☎ 679 3687 🚆 Tara Street 🚌 Cross-city buses

WHELAN'S
whelanslive.com
With good acoustics, plenty of space and a great atmosphere for live music, many up-and-coming Irish groups and overseas bands headline here. It has been licensed to serve alcohol since 1772 and renovation work revealed the original wood and stonework.
🔼 G8 ✉ 25 Wexford Street ☎ 478 0766 🚆 Pearse 🚌 16, 16A, 19, 19A, 65, 83

THE WINE CELLAR
fallonandbyrne.com
The basement of the food emporium Fallon & Byrne (▷ 37) is an informal venue, plastered with posters, with a superb selection of wines for sale. Choose from any of the bottles, with low corkage, accompanied by hearty dishes from its food menu.
🔼 G7 ✉ 11–17 Exchequer Street ☎ 472 1012 🚌 Cross-city buses

Where to Eat

777 (€€)
777.ie
This contemporary Mexican tapas res-taurant and bar serves authentic dishes such as beef *ennegrecido* and chorizo *taquitos*, with a family meal and set-menu brunch. Fabulous cocktails in the bar including plenty of margaritas.
🔼 G7 ✉ 7 Castle House, South Great George's Street ☎ 425 4052 ⏱ Lunch, brunch and dinner daily 🚌 Cross-city buses

BEAR (€–€€)
joburger.ie
A branch of the popular Jo'Burger group, the Bear is loved for its steaks with unusual salads, sides and sauces, all made using Irish ingredients. The rustic bar serves craft beers.
🔼 G7 ✉ 34–35 South William Street ☎ 474 4888 ⏱ Lunch and dinner daily 🚌 Cross-city buses

CAFÉ TOPOLIS (€€)
cafetopolis.com
Here, you can choose from pizzas cooked in a wood-burning oven, pastas, salads, seafood and meat dishes.
🔼 G7 ✉ 37 Parliament Street, Temple Bar ☎ 670 4961 ⏱ Lunch and dinner daily 🚆 Tara Street 🚌 Cross-city buses

THE CEDAR TREE (€€)

In a Middle Eastern setting, sample authentic Lebanese dishes and meze at this family-run restaurant. You can choose from a decent selection of wines from the new and old worlds, plus good Lebanese wines are served. There are also belly-dancing displays on Saturday nights.

➕ H7 ✉ 11 St. Andrew's Street ☎ 677 2121 🕐 Dinner only 🚇 Pearse 🚌 Cross-city buses

CHAMELEON (€€)

chameleonrestaurant.com

The house specialty at this Indonesian restaurant is *rijsttafel*, the traditional "rice table" with myriad dishes. Vegetarian, fish and celiac menus are also served, as well as a selection of Asian tapas if you just fancy a drink and a bite.

➕ G7 ✉ 1 Lower Fownes Street, Temple Bar ☎ 671 0362 🕐 Dinner Wed–Sat 🚇 Tara Street 🚌 Cross-city buses

CLEAVER EAST (€€€)

theclarence.ie

Irish chef Oliver Dunne has created a menu of sharing dishes and tasting plates celebrating local ingredients. It's inside the elegant Clarence, a luxury boutique hotel.

➕ G7 ✉ The Clarence, 6–8 Wellington Quay ☎ 531 3500 🕐 Lunch Fri–Sun, dinner daily 🚌 Cross-city buses

CONSIDERED (€)

dunnesstores.com

This homely café, in the hub of the stylish shopping area, is owned by beloved department store Dunnes. It's a relaxing spot, in front of huge windows, for fresh coffee and cakes, plus simple lunch dishes.

➕ G7 ✉ 42 Drury Street ☎ 677 0875 🕐 Mon–Fri 9–5 🚌 Cross-city buses

DRURY BUILDINGS (€€)

drurybuildings.com

This Italian restaurant is relatively new to Dublin's dining scene. Above the informal cocktail bar is a relaxed restaurant and tiny garden, in a sleek, homely style with reclaimed furnishings. Its menu is a delightful mix of contemporary and classic dishes, such as crab linguine and *peperoncino*, and roast halibut with fennel gratin.

➕ G7 ✉ 52–55 Drury Street ☎ 960 2095 🕐 Lunch and dinner daily 🚌 Cross-city buses

EDEN (€€)

edenbarandgrill.ie

Enjoy modern Irish food in this stylish restaurant with a huge stained-glass ceiling and a 21st-century belle epoque edge. Enjoy meaty mains such as beef bourguignon or chargrilled striploin steak, followed by a choice of unusual and interesting desserts like hazelnut chocolate soup.

➕ H7 ✉ 7 South William Street ☎ 670 6887 🕐 Lunch and dinner daily 🚇 Pearse 🚌 Cross-city buses

ELEPHANT AND CASTLE (€€)

elephantandcastle.ie

A popular place, serving one of Dublin's largest breakfast and brunch menus, with American and European favorites. Expect to have to wait in line for a table, especially on Sundays.

➕ G7 ✉ 18 Temple Bar ☎ 679 3121 🕐 Breakfast, brunch, lunch and dinner daily 🚇 Tara Street 🚌 Cross-city buses

FADE STREET SOCIAL (€€)

fadestreetsocial.com

On a small street packed with dining and nightlife spots, Dylan McGrath uses local produce to create interesting Irish and European dishes. Try braised rabbit

CELTIC COOKING

Today's Irish cooking draws inspiration from many sources, but simplicity is the key when it comes to serving fresh local produce. Smoked salmon, oysters, hearty soups and stews are readily available in most Dublin restaurants and pubs. Some adopt a traditional style, serving comfort food, such as seafood chowder and Irish stew, in settings with turf fires and local music, while others are culinary trendsetters nationally and internationally.

with white wine or a classic Irish stew and wood-fired pumpkin flatbread. There is also a tapas menu in the gastro bar.

⊞ G7 ⊠ 6 Fade Street ☎ 604 0066
🕐 Lunch Tue–Sat, dinner daily; Gastro bar: tapas daily 5pm till late ⊟ Cross-city buses

THE FUMBALLY (€)

thefumbally.ie

A group of food-loving friends set up this informal café, popular for its excellent coffee and mainly organic daily menu. Irish breakfast, Middle Eastern wraps, fresh soups and homemade cakes are on offer.

⊞ F8 ⊠ Fumbally Lane ☎ 529 8732
🕐 Breakfast and lunch (till 5pm) Tue–Sat, dinner Wed ⊟ Cross-city buses

F.X. BUCKLEY (€€€)

fxbuckley.ie

The Temple Bar branch is a meat eater's heaven, specializing in Irish grass-fed heritage steaks, with your choice of cut. You can also add seared foie gras or oysters wrapped in bacon for a more hearty dish.

⊞ G7 ⊠ 2 Crow Street, Temple Bar
☎ 671 1248 🕐 Dinner daily 🚊 Tara Street
⊟ Cross-city buses

GALLAGHERS BOXTY HOUSE (€€)

boxtyhouse.ie

Come here for traditional food focused around the boxty, an Irish potato pancake with a choice of fillings. It's also known for the tasty boxty-bread ice cream.

⊞ G7 ⊠ 20–21 Temple Bar ☎ 677 2762
🕐 Lunch and dinner daily 🚊 Tara Street
⊟ Cross-city buses

LEMON CREPE & COFFEE CO (€)

lemonco.com

Head here for mouth-watering savory and sweet crêpes and waffles, and wash them down with some great coffees.

⊞ G7 ⊠ 66 South William Street ☎ 672 9044 🕐 Daily from 8am 🚊 Pearse
⊟ Cross-city buses

LEO BURDOCK (€)

leoburdock.com

This famous "chipper" has been serving takeout fish and chips since 1913. In addition to cod and haddock, it offers jumbo tiger prawns with thick-cut chips.

⊞ G7 ⊠ 2 Werburgh Street ☎ 454 0306
🕐 Daily ⊟ Cross-city buses

MEXICO TO ROME (€)

mexicotorome.com

A choice of menus here allows you to mix Mexican with Italian, Irish and Asian dishes. It's popular and can be busy.

⊞ G7 ⊠ 23 East Essex Street ☎ 677 2727
🕐 Lunch and dinner daily 🚊 Tara Street
⊟ Cross-city buses

MONGOLIAN BARBEQUE (€)

mongolianbbq.ie

Create your own dish at this buffet of Asian ingredients. Your choice of meat, fish and vegetables, with sauces and spices, is cooked in front of you.

⊞ G7 ⊠ 7 Anglesea Street ☎ 670 4154
🕐 Lunch and dinner daily ⊟ Cross-city buses

MONTY'S OF KATMANDU (€€)

montys.ie

The city's only Nepalese restaurant, with deep-red walls and dark wood, offers intriguing South Asian dishes including Nepalese lamb masala and plenty of vegetarian side dishes.

➕ G7 ✉ 28 Eustace Street ☎ 670 4911 🕐 Lunch Mon–Sat, dinner daily 🚇 Tara Street 🚌 Cross-city buses

NEON (€–€€)

neon17.ie

It's an informal, buzzing atmosphere for dining on Asian street food. The Thai chefs create some real Southeast Asian favorites, like Singapore noodles, prawn *massaman* curry and *nasi goreng*. Dine at communal tables surrounded by urban-rustic decor.

➕ G9 ✉ 17 Camden Street Lower ☎ 405 2222 🕐 Mon–Fri from 5pm, Sat–Sun from 2pm 🚌 Cross-city buses

PICHET (€€)

pichetrestaurant.ie

Classic bistro food with top seasonal ingredients is produced here by award-winning chef Stephen Gibson. Service is good, there is a plush interior and a stylish cocktail bar.

➕ H7 ✉ 14–15 Trinity Street ☎ 677 1060 🕐 Daily lunch and dinner 🚇 Harcourt 🚌 Cross-city buses

QUEEN OF TARTS (€)

queenoftarts.ie

Delicious cakes, bakes and tarts, plus hot food for breakfast and lunch, all made on the premises, feature in this tiny traditional tea shop (bigger sister on nearby Cow's Lane).

➕ G7 ✉ Cork Hill, Dame Street ☎ 670 7499 🕐 Daily breakfast, lunch (open till 7pm) 🚇 Tara Street 🚌 Cross-city buses

---

IN VOGUE

It is essential to make reservations at the upscale and Michelin-starred restaurants. Many of these places offer excellent value early-bird menus (before 7pm). If you want to linger, check your table's not booked for a second party.

THE SHACK (€€)

shackrestaurant.ie

A cosy Temple Bar restaurant offering Irish and European dishes made using the best fresh ingredients.

➕ G7 ✉ 24 East Essex Street ☎ 679 0043 🕐 Lunch and dinner daily 🚇 Tara Street 🚌 Cross-city buses

THAI ORCHID (€€)

thaiorchiddublin.com

Spread over three floors, you will get all the established Thai specials at this restaurant, all freshly cooked and well-presented. Courteous Thai staff in traditional costume serve you, while Thai music playing in the background creates an ambiance.

➕ H6 ✉ 7 Westmoreland Street ☎ 671 9969 🕐 Lunch Mon–Sat, dinner daily 🚌 Cross-city buses

TROCADERO (€€–€€€)

trocadero.ie

Going strong since 1957, this classic venue is still a favorite of well-heeled locals. It has a long tradition as a theater restaurant, with many photos on the wall of famous faces who have dined here. European and Irish dishes use top local products, such as roast rack of Wicklow lamb. There's also a good pre-theater menu.

➕ H7 ✉ 4 St. Andrew's Street ☎ 677 5545 🕐 Mon–Sat 4.30pm till late 🚌 Cross-city buses

The area north of the River Liffey is home to O'Connell Street and off this famous thoroughfare are many of Dublin's smart shopping streets. The Docklands here are also developing rapidly.

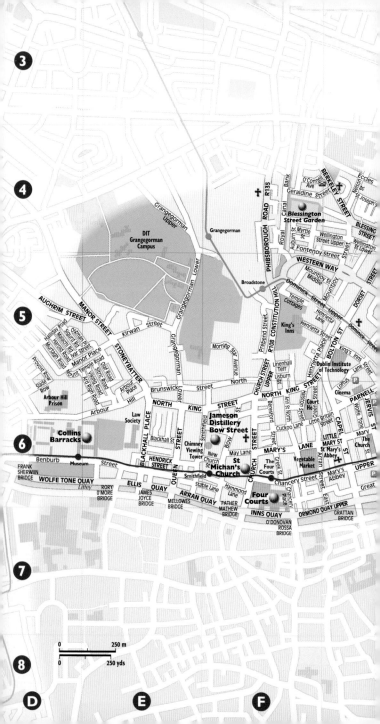

3

4

5

6

7

8

Eccles

O'Connell Ave

Geraldine Street

BERKELEY STREET

St Joseph's

Bank

R135

Royal Canal

BLESSINGTON STREET

Blessington Street Garden

Auburn St

Myrtle St

Wellington Street Upper

Wellington Street Lower

Fontenoy Street

PHIBSBOROUGH ROAD

WESTERN WAY

Mountjoy Street Middle

Mountjoy Street

DORSET STREET

Grangegorman Upper

Grangegorman

DIT Grangegorman Campus

Grangegorman Lower

Broadstone

CONSTITUTION HILL

Dominick Street Upper

Temple Cottages

Henrietta Lane

King's Inns

Henrietta Street

King's Inns Street

Dominick Street

Dublin Institute of Technology

AUGHRIM STREET

MANOR STREET

Halliday Road

Oxmantown Road

Sigurd Rd

Sitric Rd

Halpin Road

Murtagh Road

Kirwan Street

STONEYBATTER

Prebend Street

CHURCH STREET

Linenhall Terr

Lisburn St

Lurgan St

PARNELL STREET

Cinema

Mount Temple Road

Manor Place

Manor Road

Olaf Road

Viking Road

Sitric Road

Arbour Place

Brunswick Street North

NORTH KING STREET

NORTH KING STREET

Morning Star Avenue

Coleraine Street

Beresford Street

Greek Street

Little Britain Street

Green Street

Capel Street

Wolfe Tone St

JERVIS

Provost Row

Slade Row

Arbour Hill Prison

Arbour Hill

Law Society

BLACKHALL PLACE

Blackhall St

Smithfield

Jameson Distillery Bow Street

Bow Street

May Lane

Cuckoo Lane

MARY'S LANE

LITTLE MARY ST

St Mary's Abbey

Mary Street

The Church

MARY ST UPPER

Collins Barracks

Benburb Street

Museum

HENDRICK STREET

QUEEN STREET

Chimney Viewing Tower

New Church St

St Michan's Church

CHURCH STREET

The Four Courts

Chancery Street

Vegetable Market

St Mary's Abbey

Mary's Abbey

Great

FRANK SHERWIN BRIDGE

WOLFE TONE QUAY

Liffey

RORY O'MORE BRIDGE

ELLIS QUAY

JAMES JOYCE BRIDGE

MELLOWS BRIDGE

ARRAN QUAY

FATHER MATHEW BRIDGE

Stable Lane

Hammond Lane

Chancery Place

Four Courts

INNS QUAY

O'DONOVAN ROSSA BRIDGE

ORMOND QUAY UPPER

GRATTAN BRIDGE

0   250 m

0   250 yds

D   **E**   **F**

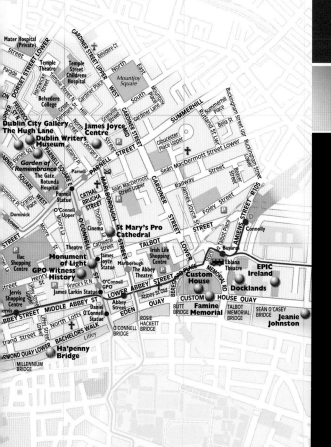

Mater Hospital
(Private)
Street
DORSET STREET LOWER
Parade
Eccles Street
Wellington Street
Upper
Temple
Theatre
Temple
Street
Childrens
Hospital
GARDINER STREET UPPER
Belvedere Ct
North
Mountjoy
Square
Belvedere
College
Hardwicke Street
Temple Street N.
Gardiner Place
Gardiner Lane
Denmark St.
Hill
South
Great
Grenville Street
GARDINER STREET MID.
SUMMERHILL
Buckingham Street Upper
Summerhill
Place
Richmond St. Lwr.
Bella St.
Buckingham Street Lower

**Dublin City Gallery
The Hugh Lane
Dublin Writers
Museum**
PARNELL SQ N.
**James Joyce
Centre**
North Great George's Street
Rutland St.
Gloucester
Place Upper
Sean MacDermott Street Lower
Street
St
Brewer
Street
Foley Street

PARNELL SQUARE WEST
Granby Row
**Garden of
Remembrance**
Dominick Pl.
Granby Place
**Parnell
Statue**
Parnell
CATHAL
BRUGHA
STREET
MARLBOROUGH
PARNELL STREET
Sean MacDermott
Street Upper
GARDINER STREET LOWER
Railway
James Joyce Street
Talbot Place
AMIENS STREET R105
Connolly
PARNELL SQUARE EAST
The Gate
Rotunda
Hospital
O'Connell
Upper
Thomas Lane

Dominick
STREET
Moore La.
Cathedral
Cinema
**St Mary's Pro
Cathedral**
TALBOT
**Irish Life
Shopping
Centre**
Store
P
Busáras
MEMORIAL RD

Theatre
Ilac
Shopping
Centre
Henry Place
**Monument
of Light**
**GPO Witness
History**
James
Joyce
Statue
O'Connell
STREET
James
Marlborough
**The Abbey
Theatre**
STREET LOWER
Beresford Place
**Eblana
Theatre**
**EPIC
Ireland**

Prince's St. N.
O'Connell
GPO
**Custom
House**
Docklands

Street
Jervis
Shopping
Centre
James Larkin Statue
LOWER ABBEY ST
ABBEY
STREET
CUSTOM HOUSE QUAY
Abbey St. Old
QUAY

ABBEY STREET
MIDDLE ABBEY ST
Jervis
Liffey Street
North Lotts
EDEN
**Daniel
O'Connell
Statue**
Abbey
Street
CUSTOM HOUSE
BUTT
BRIDGE
**Famine
Memorial**
TALBOT
MEMORIAL
BRIDGE
SEAN O'CASEY
BRIDGE
**Jeanie
Johnston**

Strand Street
BACHELORS WALK
Liffey
ROSIE
HACKETT
BRIDGE

ORMOND QUAY LOWER
O'CONNELL
BRIDGE
**Ha'penny
Bridge**
MILLENNIUM
BRIDGE

G   H   J

Collins Barracks

TOP 25

Collins Barracks contains the National Museum's collection of decorative arts

THE BASICS

museum.ie
+ E6
✉ Benburb Street
☎ 677 7444
🕐 Tue–Sat 10–5, Sun 2–5
🍴 Café
🚇 Heuston
🚌 25, 25A, 66, 67, 90; Luas Museum
♿ Very good
💷 Free
❓ Book tours in advance (inexpensive)

HIGHLIGHTS

● Old barracks building
● Fonthill vase
● What's in Store
● "The Way We Wore" exhibition
● Curator's Choice

Here you can view the decorative arts and social history collections of the National Museum—products of Irish artists and craftspeople that had been hidden from view for many years.

The building Sir Thomas Burgh (1670–1730), the architect of the Old Library in Trinity College (▷ 72–73), also designed Dublin's large Royal Barracks, just over 1.5km (a mile) outside the city. Built in 1704, on high ground overlooking the River Liffey, they were handed over in 1922 to the Irish State, which named them after Michael Collins, the revolutionary leader killed in an ambush toward the end of the Civil War. Until decommissioning in 1988, they were generally thought to be the oldest military barracks still in use anywhere in the world.

Exhibits The barracks opened as an annex to the National Museum in 1997, strengthening Dublin's cultural and historical focus. The items on display range from the 17th century up to the present day and comprise Irish silver, glass and furniture, all of which reached a high point of artistic excellence in the 18th century. Don't miss the Chinese porcelain Fonthill vase, which has managed to survive its well-documented wanderings in Asia and Europe, or the Persian and Venetian art nouveau items in the "What's In Store" collection. Permanent exhibitions include 250 years of Irish clothing and jewelry, "The Way We Wore," and a homage to the influential designer and architect Eileen Gray.

Dublin City Gallery
The Hugh Lane

Studying at the Hugh Lane (left); the gallery's 18th-century exterior (right)

Degas, Monet and Renoir are among the Impressionist artists whose paintings are on display in this gallery that also looks back over 100 years of Irish art, including paintings and stained glass.

Philanthropist The Hugh Lane Gallery fills a niche between the old masters on display in the National Gallery (▷ 67) and the ultramodern works in the Irish Museum of Modern Art (▷ 95). Built as a town house in 1763 by the Earl of Charlemont, the gallery now bears the name of Sir Hugh Lane, who drowned when the *Lusitania* sank in 1915. Before his death, Sir Hugh, who established Dublin's Municipal Gallery of Modern Art (a world first) in 1908, added a codicil to his will stating that a group of 39 of his Impressionist pictures, which were then in London, should go to Dublin. However, the codicil was unwitnessed, so London claimed the canvases and kept them until an agreement was reached in 1959 that the two cities would share them. The gallery has a program of temporary exhibitions, including retrospectives of Irish abstract art in the Sean Scully gallery. You can visit the reconstructed London studio of Francis Bacon, complete with its contents of more than 7,500 items.

Modern art Irish artists, including Osborne, Yeats, Orpen, Bacon and Le Brocquy, are well represented, and modern European artists include Beuys and Albers. There's also stained-glass pieces by Clarke, Hone and Scanlon.

THE BASICS

hughlane.ie

⊞ G5

✉ Charlemont House, Parnell Square North

☎ 222 5550

🕐 Tue–Thu 9.45–6, Fri, 9.45–5, Sat 10–5, Sun 11–5

🍽 Café

🚉 Connolly

🚌 Cross-city buses

♿ Good

🎟 Free

HIGHLIGHTS

● Impressionist paintings
● Jack Yeats, *There is no Night*
● Orpen, *Homage to Manet*
● Stained glass by Harry Clarke
● Francis Bacon's studio
● Free concerts on Sunday Jun–Sep
● The Sean Scully Gallery

Dublin Writers Museum

TOP 25

The Gallery of Writers (left); a stained-glass window pays tribute to Dublin's writers (right)

THE BASICS

writersmuseum.com
⊞ G5
✉ 18 Parnell Square North
☎ 872 2077
🕐 Mon–Sat 9.45–4.45, Sun and public hols 11–4.30
🍴 Café; Chapter One (▷ 62) restaurant in basement
🚆 Connolly
🚌 Cross-city buses
♿ Ground floor good (a few steps into the building)
💷 Moderate
❓ Excellent audio guide

HIGHLIGHTS

● Letters of Thomas Moore and Maria Edgeworth
● Yeats manuscript
● Indenture signed by Swift
● Painted ceiling and doors in the Gallery of Writers

Dublin has become the hub of a great literary tradition, and for centuries a meeting point for gifted writers. This museum celebrates their diverse talents and displays a fascinating range of the writers' memorabilia.

Great Irish writers Many languages have been spoken by Ireland's inhabitants down the centuries, but it was with the establishment of English in the 17th century that Dublin's literary reputation was founded. Restoration dramatists such as George Farquhar were followed 50 years later by the brilliance and acerbic wit of Jonathan Swift. The late 19th century saw the emergence of Oscar Wilde, whose epigrams enthralled the world. William Butler Yeats, encouraged by the flourishing Irish literary movement, helped found the Abbey Theatre, which opened in 1904. His contemporary, George Bernard Shaw, and subsequent writers such as James Joyce, Samuel Beckett and Brendan Behan have continued to open new horizons in world literature.

Displays Photographs, paintings and other items linked with Ireland's literary titans are backed up with lots of explanatory material. First editions and rare volumes abound, and there are original letters of the poet Thomas Moore, a manuscript of W.B. Yeats and an indenture signed by Jonathan Swift. The building itself, an 18th-century mansion, is rather spectacular.

EPIC Ireland is a
21st-century sensory
spectacle

TOP
25

EPIC Ireland

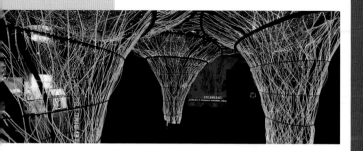

EPIC Ireland is a 21st-century visitor experience in a former 19th-century wine and tobacco warehouse. In a series of spaces and displays in brick-lined vaults, an audio-visual feast tells the story of the Irish diaspora.

Sculptures and displays Themed around the astounding fact that the Irish diaspora is one of the world's largest, the 20 immersive galleries tell of the many millions of people who left Ireland due to dramatic events such as the Famine in the mid-19th century. A huge, striking sculpture depicts the history of the epic sea journeys that they made over the centuries. Elsewhere in the subterranean galleries, a series of interactive exhibitions, with touch screens, sound and installations, have four themes: Migration, Motivation, Influence and Connection. One section looks at famous people of Irish descent including JFK, Billy the Kid, Grace Kelly and Charles de Gaulle. There is also a part devoted to Irish music and dance and how its influences have reached around the world. The CHQ Building (▷ 59) has its own history and was the location for the 1856 Crimean War Banquet.

Genealogy section Part of EPIC Ireland is the Irish Family History Centre, where visitors can search for their Irish ancestors using the latest digital technology. Visitors can have a 15-minute consultation with a genealogy expert and use the interactive displays to research their heritage.

THE BASICS

epicchq.com
✚ J6
✉ CHQ Building, Custom House Quay
☎ 531 3688
🕐 Daily 10–5
🚊 Connolly
🚌 Cross-city buses; Luas George's Dock
♿ Excellent
💷 Expensive
❓ Gift shop

HIGHLIGHTS

● Ship voyage sculpture
● Irish music footage
● Sporting heroes exhibits
● Famous faces

GPO Witness History

GPO Witness History brings alive the dramatic events that took place in 1916

THE BASICS

gpowitnesshistory.ie

➕ H6

✉ GPO, O'Connell Street

☎ 872 1916

🕐 Mon–Fri 9–5.30, Sat–Sun 10–5.30. Last admission 4.30

🍴 Café

🚌 Cross-city buses; Luas Abbey Street

♿ Good

💰 Expensive

1916 Tour—Beyond Barricades

✉ Dublin Bus Head Office, 59 Upper O'Connell Street

☎ 703 3024

🕐 Tue, Fri–Sun 11.30, 2.30

🚌 Cross-city buses; Luas Abbey Street

💰 Expensive

HIGHLIGHTS

● *Fire and Steel* movie
● Bullet holes in pillars
● Copy of the 1916 Proclamation of the Irish Republic

The General Post Office building, in a prominent spot on broad O'Connell Street, symbolizes the birthplace of modern Ireland and was the scene of momentous events in Ireland's political history.

Scene of siege The historic building was designed by Francis Johnston (1814), with statues by John Smith that dominate the sky-line. Inside, the reading of the Proclamation of the Irish Republic took place during the Easter Rising of 1916. The insurgents were forced to surrender after the interior was reduced to rubble—bullet holes on the portico columns are a reminder of the bitter struggle—and 16 insurgents were later executed.

Exhibition The main building is still a working post office, but its north side now houses the GPO Witness History exhibition, a permanent visitor attraction. With immersive exhibits, documents, photos and film footage, this re-creates the events that took place here during the momentous Easter Week. Don't miss the excellent short film, *Fire and Steel*, which uses original photographs and re-created scenes of events that took place in and around the GPO on that fateful day. It reflects events on both sides of the conflict, through the eyes of bystanders caught in the crossfire. On the wall is a rare copy of the 1916 proclamation. Guided tours taking in the prominent landmarks and conflict scenes of Easter Monday leave from the nearby Dublin Bus Head Office.

You will find all things Joycean at the James Joyce Centre

TOP 25

James Joyce Centre

Of all those to grace the Dublin scene during the 20th century, James Joyce has undoubtedly earned the greatest reputation internationally, so it is fitting that a whole house is devoted to the writer.

Connections This beautifully restored 18th-century house, in an impressive street of Georgian redbrick residences just 275m (300yds) from O'Connell Street, is home to the James Joyce Centre. Initially, its Joycean connection was established through a dancing master called Denis J. Maginni, who leased one of the rooms in the house around the turn of the 20th century and appears as a character in *Ulysses*. Tours are available around the house and give the opportunity to listen to tapes of "Uncle James," reading from *Ulysses* and *Finnegans Wake*.

Memorabilia Start your visit on the top floor of the building where there's an atmospheric display of re-created period rooms, videos and computer installations, as well as a whole host of items relating to Joyce's life and work, including furniture from the Paris apartment where he lived when he worked on his masterpiece, *Finnegans Wake*. Don't miss the front door out in the courtyard, rescued from the now demolished No. 7 Eccles Street, Leopold Bloom's address in *Ulysses*. The venue is a starting point for an 80- to 90-minute walking tour (payable separately) of Joycean sites on the north side of the city.

THE BASICS

jamesjoyce.ie

➕ H5

✉ 35 North Great George's Street

☎ 878 8547

🕐 Mon–Sat 10–5, Sun 12–5; closed Mon Oct–Mar

🍴 Café

🚇 Connolly

🚌 Cross-city buses

♿ Few

💷 Moderate

❓ Guided tours of house and Joycean Dublin

HIGHLIGHTS

● Joyce family members
● Recordings
● Library
● Portraits of characters in *Ulysses*
● No. 7 Eccles Street door
● Copy of Joyce's death mask

THE NORTH TOP 25

Jameson Distillery Bow St.

HIGHLIGHTS

● Whiskey tasting from the barrel
● Immersive guided tours
● Historic 18th-century building
● JJs Bar

Reopened in March 2017 after major restoration, this historical landmark was formerly known as Old Jameson Distillery. As its old name suggests, it sits in the original whiskey distillery buildings, dating back to 1780.

History With brick walls, the original stills and immense vats, a visit here is a step back in time through one of Ireland's most popular products. Jameson was the country's most famous distillery, in operation from 1780 to 1971, until it transferred to the Midleton Distillery in Cork. John Jameson, who was from Scotland, and his son (also John) became manager of the family brewery belonging to his wife, Mary Stein. The original equipment showcases the method in which whiskey was, and is still, produced.

Clockwise from far left: Barrels bear the name of this famous distillery; enter the original Jameson buildings to learn about the whiskey distilling process as it was in the 18th century to the modern methods of today

Tours and tastings Jameson's new-look attraction features cutting-edge technology—in complete contrast to its historic surroundings. It now has a choice of fully immersive guided tours: the Bow St. Experience focuses on Jameson's rich heritage; the Whiskey Makers and the Whiskey Shakers tours give more of an insight into the drink itself, including whiskey and cocktail masterclasses. Each one invites visitors to touch, taste and smell the precious product. A highlight of the "Makers" and "Shakers" tours is a visit to the live Maturation Warehouse, a crucial part of the process where you can taste the Jameson straight from the barrel. The guides will explain how, although both Ireland and Scotland both claim to have produced the very first whiskey, the Irish version is unique in its triple distillation.

THE BASICS

➕ F6
✉ Bow Street, Smithfield
☎ 807 2355
🕐 Mon–Sat 9–6, Sun 10–5
🍽 Restaurant, café and bar
🚌 Cross-city buses; Luas Smithfield
♿ Good
👖 Expensive
ℹ Gift shop

55

More to See

BLESSINGTON STREET GARDEN

A 10-minute walk from O'Connell Street is the former city reservoir, Blessington Street Basin. Here you will find a quiet haven of peace for visitors and local wildlife. Land-scaped in the mid-1990s, it is bounded by stone walls and along the pathway there are several sitting benches that face the watercourse. This little park is known as Dublin's secret garden.

➕ F4 ✉ Blessington Street ☎ 888 2538
🕐 Daily daylight hours 🚌 10 ♿ Good
🎫 Free

CUSTOM HOUSE

Designed by James Gandon in 1791, the Custom House is an outstanding example of Georgian architecture and one of Dublin's finest buildings. Burned down by the IRA in 1921, it has now been beautifully restored.

➕ J6 ✉ Custom House Quay ☎ 888 2538
🕐 Mon–Fri 10–1, 2–4 🚌 Tara Street
🚌 Cross-city buses; Luas Busáras ♿ Good
🎫 Inexpensive

DOCKLANDS

docklands.ie

The redevelopment of the former docks stretches from the Custom House east along the north of the Liffey to North Wall Quay, with developments on the south bank, too. They are linked by the Sean O' Casey Bridge (2005) and the Samuel Beckett Bridge (2010). Homes, offices, cultural venues, shops, hotels and restaurants are changing the face of the city.

➕ J6–M6 ✉ North of the Liffey 🚌 Tara Street 🚌 Cross-city buses; Luas Connolly Station

FAMINE MEMORIAL

A series of emaciated figures along the quays commemorates the Great Famine of 1845–49, a dev-astating period in Irish history when around 1 million people died. The sculptures were created by Dublin artist Rowan Gillespie. Look for the World Poverty Stone nearby.

➕ J6 ✉ Custom House Quay 🚌 Tara Street 🚌 Cross-city buses; Luas Busáras

The statue Children of Lír

The copper dome of the Custom House

FOUR COURTS

Home to the Irish law courts since 1796, the Four Courts has much in common with the Custom House—primarily its designer, James Gandon. This Dublin landmark also suffered fire damage during the turbulent events of 1921. Visits are only permitted when courts are in session.

F6 ✉ Inns Quay ☎ 888 6000
🚌 Cross-city buses; Luas Four Courts
♿ Few 🎟 Free

GARDEN OF REMEMBRANCE

The statue of the *Children of Lír* is the focal point of this contemplative garden, dedicated to those who died in pursuit of Irish independence. A poignant Irish fairy tale, about three children turned into swans by a wicked stepmother, inspired Oisín Kelly's bronze sculpture (1971).

G5 ✉ Garden of Remembrance, Parnell Square East ☎ 821 3021 🚌 Cross-city buses

JEANIE JOHNSTON

jeaniejohnston.ie

This is an authentic replica of the *Jeanie Johnston*, a tall ship that made 16 journeys from Ireland to North America between 1847 and 1855, carrying around 2,500 poverty-stricken Irish emigrants. On board, today's visitors can see re-created scenes from those challenging journeys in the cramped sleeping quarters and on the once-crowded deck.

J/K6 ✉ Custom House Quay, North Dock ☎ 473 0111 🕐 Daily daylight hours
🚆 Tara Street 🚌 Cross-city buses; Luas George's Dock 🎟 Expensive

MONUMENT OF LIGHT

Known as the Spire, the striking edifice was unveiled in 2003 and is a prominent landmark. Standing at 120m (394ft) high, and made of reflective stainless steel which changes hue throughout the day and night, it stands on the site where Nelson's Column used to be, across the road from the General Post Office (▷ 52).

H6 ✉ O'Connell Street 🚌 Cross-city buses; Luas Abbey Street

ST. MARY'S PRO CATHEDRAL

procathedral.ie

Mother church for Catholic Dublin, affectionately known as "the Pro," this impressive 1825 building has hosted many Church and State occasions. Sunday mass is sung by the Palestrina Choir.

H5 ✉ Marlborough Street ☎ 874 5441
🕐 Mon–Fri 7.30–6.45, Sat 7.30–7.15, Sun 9–1.45, 5.30–7.45, public hols 10–1.30
🚌 Cross-city buses; Luas Abbey Street

ST. MICHAN'S CHURCH

procathedral.ie

A functioning parish church, St. Michan's is best known for its burial vaults. Here lie the mummified remains of some of Dublin's famous—and infamous—characters from the 17th to 19th centuries, including earls and a Crusader. Bram Stoker, creator of Dracula, was said to have visited here with his family. There are regular tours of the vaults and church, which contains a pipe organ.

F6 ✉ Church Road ☎ 872 4154
🕐 Mid-Mar to Oct daily 10–12.45, 2–4.30; Nov to mid-Mar 12.30–3.30 🚌 Cross-city buses; Luas Four Courts

A Walk North of the River

This walk is in the lesser-known northern district of Dublin, undergoing a major rejuvenation. It also takes in part of the quays.

DISTANCE: 2km (1.25 miles) **ALLOW:** 1 hour plus stops

START

GRESHAM HOTEL (▷ 112)
✚ H5 ⬛ Cross-city buses

END

JAMESON DISTILLERY BOW ST.
(▷ 54) ✚ F6 ⬛ 68, 69, 79, 90;
Luas Smithfield

❶ Start at the Gresham Hotel (▷ 112) on O'Connell Street. Facing the hotel turn right and walk south on O'Connell Street toward the quayside.

❷ Continue to the General Post Office (▷ 52) and then look up for the "Spire" (▷ 57), which towers above the street and sways gently in the breeze.

❸ Opposite the Spire go left into pedestrian Henry Street. Halfway down is the Ilac shopping mall (▷ 59), with the Jervis Centre (▷ 59) a little further along. Turn onto Mary Street.

❹ Continue along Mary Street and at the T-junction at the end turn left into Capel Street. Walk on over two roads down to the quayside.

❽ At the end turn right into Bow Street where you will find Jameson Distillery Bow St. (▷ 54). You can pause here to take a tour, sample a glass of whiskey or have coffee or lunch. Here, too, is Duck Lane, with popular restaurants.

❼ Take the next right, Church Street. Cross the road and you will see St. Michan's Church (▷ 57) on your left, famous for the mummified bodies in its crypt. Continue to the traffic lights and turn left into May Lane.

❻ To your right is the fine Georgian building of the Four Courts (▷ 57).

❺ In front of you is the Grattan Bridge with its fine sculpted sea horses. Turn right along the quay, passing the next bridge, O'Donovan Rossa Bridge, and into Inns Quay.

Shopping

ARNOTTS
arnotts.ie
Ireland's largest department store, opened in 1843, stocks everything fashionable in clothes, interiors, household, leisure, entertainment and cosmetics.
➕ G6 ✉ 12 Henry Street ☎ 805 0400
🚉 Connolly 🚌 Cross-city buses; Luas Jervis

THE CHQ BUILDING
chq.ie
A 19th-century wine and tobacco store is now a mall of smart boutiques, shops, coffee bars and Mitchell & Sons, Dublin's oldest fine wine merchants.
➕ J6 ✉ IFSC, George's Dock ☎ 673 6054
🚉 Tara Street 🚌 Cross-city buses; Luas Busáras

DUBLIN WRITERS MUSEUM BOOKSHOP
writersmuseum.com
This excellent shop covers all aspects of Irish writing from travel to poetry, including works by many of the writers featured in the museum.
➕ G5 ✉ 18 Parnell Street North ☎ 872 2077 🚉 Connolly 🚌 Cross-city buses

EASON
eason.ie
This vast bookstore has a huge selection of books and magazines together with stationery, art equipment and music. There is also a café.
➕ H6 ✉ 40 Lower O'Connell Street ☎ 858 3800 🚉 Tara Street or Connolly 🚌 Cross-city buses

ILAC CENTRE
ilac.ie
Dublin's longest-established shopping mall is a labyrinth of small shops and high street names such as Dunnes.
➕ G6 ✉ Henry Street ☎ 828 8900 🚉 Tara Street 🚌 Cross-city buses; Luas Jervis

JERVIS CENTRE
jervis.ie
Popular with Dubliners, this modern mall is spread over several floors. It has more than 60 shops, of Irish, UK and European retailers, including Topshop and Bershka, plus a food court.
➕ G6 ✉ 125 Abbey Street Upper ☎ 878 1323 🚉 Tara Street 🚌 Cross-city buses; Luas Jervis

LOUIS COPELAND
louiscopeland.com
This is the flagship store of the renowned gentlemen's outfitter with suits, coats, shirts and ties. A Louis Copeland suit, made to measure or off the peg, is a rite of passage for well-dressed Irish men.
➕ G6 ✉ 39–41 Capel Street ☎ 872 1600
🚉 Tara Street 🚌 Cross-city buses

WINDING STAIR
winding-stair.com
A literary landmark overlooking Ha'penny Bridge, this atmospheric independent bookstore offers a wide range of new and second-hand books. There is also a delightful restaurant upstairs (▷ 62).
➕ G6 ✉ 40 Lower Ormond Quay ☎ 872 6576 🚉 Tara Street 🚌 Cross-city buses

CRAFTSMANSHIP
Dublin's rich reputation as a hub of creative excellence dates back several centuries. Irish furniture and silver of the Georgian period embody some of the finest craftsmanship of the late 18th and early 19th centuries (the harp in the hallmark indicates a piece was made in Ireland), and early 20th-century Irish art has attracted worldwide acclaim. Antiques fairs take place regularly.

Entertainment and Nightlife

3ARENA

3arena.ie

A state-of-the-art entertainment venue in Docklands, formerly known as The 02. Top names in music and comedy appear, plus musicals, opera and concerts. This is Dublin's star-studded attraction, and tickets sell fast.

➕ M6 ✉ North Wall Quay ☎ 819 8888 🚌 151; Luas Docklands Station

ABBEY THEATRE

abbeytheatre.ie

Founded in 1904, the national theater played a vital role in the renaissance of Irish culture in the ensuing years. Today, the quality of the performances and playwriting of Irish works is world-class. Many first runs go on to grace the stages of New York's Broadway or London's West End.

➕ H6 ✉ 26 Abbey Street Lower ☎ 878 7222 🚆 Connolly/Tara Street 🚌 Cross-city buses

THE COBBLESTONE

cobblestonepub.ie

A traditional pub with regular music sessions, including Irish, blues and folk, this bar has been a Smithfield fixture for many years. There are nightly sessions, plus afternoon music at weekends.

➕ E6 ✉ 77 King Street North ☎ 872 1799 🚌 Cross-city buses; Luas Smithfield

GATE THEATRE

gate-theatre.ie

Some of Dublin's most inspired and sophisticated plays are performed in this 18th-century building. The theater's actors, playwrights and productions have an international reputation and tour the world.

➕ G5 ✉ Cavendish Row, Parnell Square ☎ 874 4045 🚆 Connolly 🚌 Cross-city buses

GRAND CENTRAL

louisfitzgerald.com

This elegant café-bar is converted from a 1920s banking hall, with columns and a huge dome. It has beers on tap, wines and a lunchtime menu.

➕ H6 ✉ 10–11 O'Connell Street ☎ 872 8658 🚌 Cross-city buses; Luas Abbey Street

THE GRAND SOCIAL

thegrandsocial.ie

Live bands of many genres and club nights fill this popular four-level music venue. The Ballroom, downstairs, is a huge space for DJ events, with the cozy Parlour Bar overlooking Ha'penny Bridge. It hosts the weekly Ha'penny Bridge Flea Market (Saturday noon–6).

➕ G6 ✉ 35 Lower Liffey Street ☎ 874 0076 🚌 Cross-city buses; Luas Jervis

LAUGHTER LOUNGE

laughterlounge.com

Treat yourself to a good giggle with a host of local and international stand-up talent on Thursday, Friday and Saturday.

➕ H6 ✉ 4–8 Eden Quay ☎ 878 3003 🚆 Tara Street 🚌 Cross-city buses

LIGHTHOUSE CINEMA

lighthousecinema.ie

This independent cinema has most of the latest major releases, plus an interesting selection of short films and

---

DANCE

When looking for the best clubs in Dublin, go by the name of that particular night at the club rather than the name of the venue itself. Most good dance nights are independently run gigs organized by promoters. *The Event Guide* has the most comprehensive and accurate listings or ask at the Tourist Information Office.

a program of live screenings of opera, ballet and theater performances. It is one of the venues for the Dublin International Film Festival.

🔶 E6 ✉ Market Square, Smithfield ☎ 872 8006 🚌 Cross-city buses; Luas Smithfields

PANTI BAR
pantibar.com
One of the first gay bars in Dublin, Panti Bar is all about neon, scarlet decor and naughty entertainment on its two floors. There is live entertainment most nights, from DJs to cabaret acts and drag shows.

🔶 G6 ✉ 7–8 Capel Street ☎ 874 0710 🚌 Cross-city buses; Luas Jervis

RYAN'S
fxbuckley.ie
A landmark 19th-century pub filled with original mahogany snugs, etched mirrors and gas lamps. Past drinkers include American presidents Bush Sr. and Jr.,

plus JFK. There's a full gastro bar menu with oysters and steak.

🔶 D6 ✉ 28 Parkgate Street ☎ 677 6097 🚌 Cross-city buses; Luas Museum

VOODOO LOUNGE
A funky bar-club, this venue has eclectic voodoo-themed decor and stages decent independent bands on its small stage, favoring indie, garage and metal music. The bar is open until late.

🔶 E6 ✉ 39 Arran Quay ☎ 873 6013 🚌 Cross-city buses; Luas Smithfield

WIGWAM
wigwamdublin.ie
It's a café-bar by day, but by night it is a cocktail bar, with a choice of more than 100 types of rum, good craft ales and wine. There's a roof terrace, and DJ club in the basement, open late.

🔶 G6 ✉ 54 Middle Abbey Street ☎ 873 4020 🚌 Cross-city buses; Luas Jervis

Where to Eat

PRICES
Prices are approximate, based on a 3-course meal for one person.
€€€ over €50
€€ €30–€50
€ under €30

BESHOFF'S (€)
beshoffrestaurant.com
Great fish and chips with catch-of-the-day specials at this Dublin institution. Grab a window seat for views of busy O'Connell Street.

🔶 H6 ✉ 6 Upper O'Connell Street

☎ 872 4400 🍽 Breakfast, lunch and dinner daily 🚉 Connolly 🚌 Cross-city buses; Luas Abbey Street

LE BON CRUBEEN (€€)
leboncrubeen.ie
The brasserie menu here is always top class. Top ingredients from Irish suppliers help to create European-influenced dishes. There is a pre-theater menu, handy for those heading to the Gate or 3Arena.

🔶 H5 ✉ 81–82 Talbot Street ☎ 704 0126 🍽 Lunch and dinner daily 🚉 Connolly 🚌 Cross-city buses; Luas Connolly

BROTHER HUBBARD (€–€€)

brotherhubbard.ie

Relaxed and informal, Middle Eastern dishes are the specialty here, with home-made cakes in the afternoon. It's furnished with stools and wooden tables, with banquettes and exposed brick adding to the atmosphere.

🚩 G6 ✉ 153 Capel Street ☎ 441 1112 ⓘ Breakfast and lunch Mon–Fri, brunch Sat–Sun, dinner Wed–Sat 🚆 Connolly 🚌 Cross-city buses; Luas Abbey Street

CHAPTER ONE (€€€)

chapteronerestaurant.com

One of Dublin's most elegant restaurants is within the basement of the Dublin Writers' Museum. Irish contemporary food meets French classic cooking. There is a good wine vault.

🚩 G5 ✉ 18–19 Parnell Square ☎ 873 2266 ⓘ Lunch Tue–Fri, dinner Tue–Sat 🚆 Connolly 🚌 Cross-city buses

ELY BAR & BRASSERIE (€€)

elywinebar.ie

Located inside stone-walled wine vaults, Ely's stocks an enviable collection of wines and offers an extensive menu of contemporary Irish meat and fish dishes. There is also a waterside terrace.

🚩 J6 ✉ CHQ Building, George's Dock ☎ 672 0010 ⓘ Daily noon–late 🚌 Cross-city buses; Luas Connolly

HARBOURMASTER BAR & RESTAURANT (€€–€€€)

harbourmaster.ie

In a waterside setting, this is an old-style pub with a modern dining room serving wholesome Irish food, ranging from pan-fried scallops to rump of lamb.

🚩 J6 ✉ Custom House Dock ☎ 670 1688 ⓘ Lunch, dinner daily 🚆 Connolly 🚌 Luas Busáras

MV CILL AIRNE (€€)

mvcillairne.com

Historic little ship moored in Docklands, in Quay 16, with a good restaurant serving European dishes, plus a bistro and bar. Convenient for the 3Arena.

🚩 K6 ✉ Quay 16, North Wall Quay ☎ 817 8760 ⓘ Daily lunch and dinner 🚆 Docklands Station 🚌 Luas Busáras

THE WINDING STAIR (€€)

winding-stair.com

Overlooking the river, and above the bookshop of the same name (▷ 59), this smart restaurant serves wholesome dishes such as Irish seafood chowder and roasted Kerry venison.

🚩 G6 ✉ 40 Ormond Quay Lower ☎ 872 7320 ⓘ Daily lunch and dinner 🚆 Tara Street 🚌 Cross-city buses; Luas Jervis

THE WOOLLEN MILLS (€€)

thewoollenmills.com

Overlooking the Liffey, the informal restaurant in a historic building is spread over four floors, including a roof terrace. In addition to its all-day menu of casual Irish dishes, there's also a bakery and pizza oven on site.

🚩 G6 ✉ 42 Ormond Quay Lower ☎ 828 0835 ⓘ Daily lunch and dinner 🚌 Cross-city buses; Luas Jervis

YAMAMORI (€€)

yamamori.ie

One of four branches of the small Japanese chain, this Northside outlet has 19th-century Japanese artifacts and a bamboo garden. Specializing in sushi and *nigiri*, the excellent menu is diverse, with a huge choice of tempura, teriyaki and ramen dishes.

🚩 G6 ✉ 38–39 Ormond Quay Upper ☎ 872 0003 ⓘ Daily noon–late 🚌 Cross-city buses; Luas Jervis

This district, south of the River Liffey, has been Dublin's most elegant and fashionable area since the 18th century. Here you will find Trinity College, the national museums and elegant Georgian squares.

5
6
7
8
9

ROSIE
HACKETT
BRIDGE
BUTT
BRIDGE
TALBOT
MEMORIAL
BRIDGE
SEÁN
O'CASEY
BRIDGE

O'CONNELL
BRIDGE

BURGH QUAY

GEORGE'S QUAY

D'OLIER STREET

Hawkins St

Poolbeg
Street

Cinema

TARA STREET

Luke St

TARA
STREET
STATION

D

Moss Street

Gloucester Street
South

TOWNSEND

STREET

COLLEGE ST

Trinity

PEARSE

Mark's Street

Mark's Lane

STREET

Trinity College

Irish
Whiskey
Museum

Douglas Hyde
Gallery

GRAFTON ST

NASSAU STREET

LEINSTER STREET SOUTH

College
Park

Dental
Hospital

LINCOLN PLACE

WESTLAND ROW

Oscar
Wilde's
House

Dawson

Duke St

DAWSON ST

Powerscourt
Shopping Centre

Clarendon Street

Grafton Street

Anne St S

Chatham Street

School
of Music

King St South

MOLESWORTH
ST

S Frederick Street

Setana Pl

Schoolhouse
Lane

KILDARE ST

National
Library

Leinster
House

CLARE STREET

National
Gallery of
Ireland

WEST

Oscar
Wilde
Statue

St Ann's Church

Gaiety
Theatre

Royal Irish
Academy
Library

Mansion House

National
Museum of
Ireland

Natural History
Museum

SOUTH

MERRION STREET UPPER

Fitzwilliam Lane

Mercer Street

Glovers

St Stephen's
Green Centre

Alley

Stephen's Green

WEST

NORTH

Royal
Fusilier's
Arch

Viking
Splash
Tours

The Little
Museum
of Dublin

Shelbourne
Hotel

MERRION ROW

York Street

The Royal
College of
Surgeons

EAST

Hume
Street

Ely Place

Ely
Lane

BAGGOT

Mercer
Lane

CUFFE STREET

St Stephen's
Green

SOUTH

RHA
Gallagher
Gallery

Ely
House

PEMBROKE STREET LOWER

FITZWILLIAM ST UPR

Montague
Street

Newman
University
Church

Newman
House

Iveagh
House

TERRACE

Leeson
Lane

Laverty
Court

Quinn's Lane

PEMBROKE ST UPPER

North

Pembroke
Lane

Fitzwilliam
Square
South

FITZWILLIAM PLACE EAST

Camden
Place

Stable
Lane

Iveagh
Gardens

National
Concert Hall

University
College

EARLSFORT

LEESON STREET LOWER

PEMBROKE STREET LOWER

Leeson
Close

Kingram
Place

Cumberland
Road

Lad Lane

Lad Lane Upr

HARCOURT

STREET

HATCH STREET UPPER

Hatch Street Lower

Hatch Place

Eye & Ear
Hospital

Leeson
Place

R738

Wilton

MESPIL

ADELAIDE

ROAD

EUSTACE
BRIDGE

G
H
J

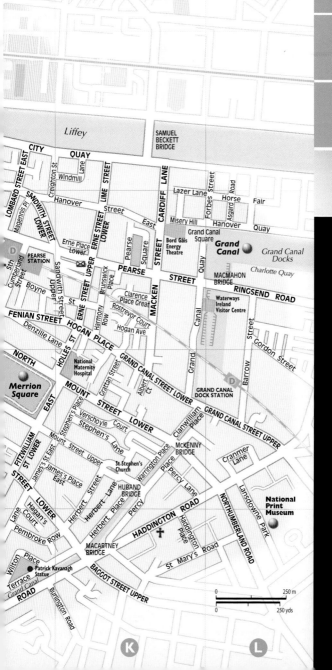

Liffey

SAMUEL
BECKETT
BRIDGE

CITY   QUAY

LOMBARD STREET EAST
SANDWITH STREET LOWER
Magennis Pl
Creighton St
Windmill
Lane
HANOVER
Street
LIME STREET
CARDIFF LANE
Lazer Lane
Forbes Street
Asgard Road
Horse   Fair

ERNE STREET LOWER
East
Misery Hill   Hanover   Quay
Erne Place Lower
Grand Canal
Square
Bord Gáis
Energy
Theatre

Grand Canal   Grand Canal
Docks

D
PEARSE
STATION
Sth
Cumberland
Street
Boyne
SANDWITH STREET UPPER
ERNE STREET UPPER
Brunswick
Place
Pearse
square
PEARSE   STREET   MACKEN
Charlotte Quay
MACMAHON
BRIDGE
RINGSEND   ROAD

FENIAN STREET
HOGAN PLACE
Denzille Lane
HOLLES ST
Harmony Row
Clarence
Place Great
Rostrevor Court
Hogan Ave
Quay
Grand Canal
Waterways
Ireland
Visitor Centre
Gordon   Street
Barrow   Street

NORTH
*Merrion
Square*
MOUNT
MERRION SQUARE EAST
Grattan Street
Albert Ct
GRAND CANAL STREET LOWER
National
Maternity
Hospital
GRAND CANAL
DOCK STATION

D

FITZWILLIAM ST LOWER
Stephen's Place
Verschoyle
Court
Stephen's Lane
Mount Street Upper
STREET   LOWER
Clanwilliam
Place
GRAND CANAL STREET UPPER
MCKENNY
BRIDGE
Cranmer
Lane

James's st East
James's Place
East
St.Stephen's
Church
HUBAND
BRIDGE
Warrington Place
Percy Place
Percy Lane
NORTHUMBERLAND ROAD
Lansdowne Park

*National
Print
Museum*

STREET
LOWER
Hagan's
Court
Herbert Street
Herbert Lane
Herbert Place
Percy
HADDINGTON   ROAD
Haddington
Place

Pembroke Row
MACARTNEY
BRIDGE
St Mary's   Road

Wilton   Place
*Patrick Kavanagh
Statue*
Terrace
Grand Canal
ROAD
Burlington Road
BAGGOT STREET UPPER

0 _____ 250 m
0 _____ 250 yds

K   L

The Little Museum of Dublin

TOP 25

Discover all things good, bad or fascinating about 20th-century Dublin at this pint-size museum

THE BASICS

littlemuseum.ie

H8

✉ 15 St. Stephen's Green

🕐 Daily 9.30–5, Thu 9.30–8

☎ 661 1000

🚌 Cross-city buses; Luas St. Stephen's Green

♿ Good

💷 Moderate

❓ Guided tours only, hourly

HIGHLIGHTS

● 1916 Uprising photos
● Letter written by James Joyce in 1902
● Soccer photos

This gem of a museum is a collection of myriad items telling the story of the Irish capital through its people. Its launch was preceded with an appeal to the public to donate 20th-century historical objects relating to the city, and the response was overwhelming.

Photos and documents Guided tours take you through the history of Dublin over the previous century, from photographs of Queen Victoria's visit in 1900, to the global pop sensation of U2. You'll also find exhibits about the 1907 International Exhibition in Herbert Park, and photos showing the desperate poverty of some of Dublin's tenement housing. There is fascinating material from the 1916 Uprising, including a souvenir propoganda placard. Also on show is a first edition copy of James Joyce's classic novel *Ulysses*, and the slightly more morbid display of his death mask from 1941.

Sports stars Photos also tell the story of Ireland's sporting achievements, including a photo of the Ireland soccer team before they played against Hungary—and posing the question of were they giving a fascist salute?—and Ireland's most successful team, Shamrock Rovers FC, complete with their striped shirts and socks from 1954. More recent exhibits include a certificate giving Mother Teresa the Freedom of Dublin, and Bill Clinton's letter to Gerry Adams granting him a visa to the United States.

The Millennium Wing, added a decade ago and fronting onto Clare Street, is an exciting exhibition space

National Gallery

The National Gallery enjoys considerable standing on the international scene as the home of one of Europe's premier collections of old masters.

Origins Facing onto Merrion Square, the gallery is set in relaxing green surroundings. It was established in 1854 and opened in 1864 to display old master paintings to inspire budding Irish artists of the mid-Victorian period. Its contents have expanded 20-fold in the century-and-a-half since then, helped by many bequests. These include works by Vermeer, Velázquez and Murillo; the legacy of one-third of George Bernard Shaw's residual estate enabled the gallery to acquire important works by Fragonard and J.L. David, among others.

Masterpieces The Irish paintings show a progression from the 18th century onward while the old masters, for which the gallery is famous, are on an upper floor. Wide coverage is given to most European schools of painting—including icons, early Italians (Uccello and Fra Angelico), Renaissance (Titian, Tintoretto), Dutch and Flemish (Rembrandt, Rubens), Spanish (Goya), French (Poussin) and British (Reynolds and Raeburn, among others). The display also covers Impressionists and modern painters up to Picasso. One room is devoted to watercolors and drawings—including 31 by Turner, shown every January. The Millennium Wing houses an area for the study of Irish art and temporary exhibition galleries.

HIGHLIGHTS

- Yeats Archive
- Fra Angelico, *Attempted Martyrdom of SS Cosmas and Damian*
- Titian, *Ecce Homo*
- Vermeer, *A Lady Writing*
- Rembrandt, *Rest on the Flight into Egypt*
- Van Gogh, *Rooftops in Paris*
- Picasso, *Still Life with a Mandolin*
- Millennium Wing

HIGHLIGHTS

● Prehistoric gold
● Tara Brooch
● Ardagh Chalice
● Cross of Cong
● Tully Lough Cross
● Viking exhibition
● Egyptian room

TIP

● Many of the treasures of this museum are now on show at Collins Barracks (▷ 48) and worth the 2km (1.25-mile) trip.

This branch of the National Museum houses most of Ireland's greatest archeological treasures. A visit here is a must for a deeper understanding of the country's prehistoric history and culture.

Extensive collections For more than a century, the twin institutions of the National Museum (1890) and the National Library have faced each other across the square leading to the Dáil, or Houses of Parliament. At ground-level, the museum has displays of Western Europe's most extensive collection of prehistoric gold ornaments, mostly dating from the Bronze Age (c1500–500BC). The torcs and jewelry are stunning, as are the brooches, crosses and croziers (AD600–1200), from Ireland's early Christian monasteries, on show in the Treasury.

Among the greatest gems here are the eighth-century Tara Brooch, the Ardagh Chalice and the Derrynaflan Hoard. Don't miss the rare Tully Lough Cross, an Irish altar cross of the eighth or ninth century. Discovered in Roscommon in fragments, it has been meticulously reconstructed. The discovery of two Iron Age bog bodies in 2003 led to a radical new theory that linked them with sovereignty rituals, as the "Kingship and Sacrifice" exhibition explains.

History Upstairs, "Viking Ireland" spans AD795–1170. It documents invasions, trades and crafts and has scale models of Viking Dublin. "Medieval Ireland" covers life from the 12th century Anglo-Norman invasion to the Reformation. Further exhibitions feature items from Ancient Cyprus and Ancient Egypt.

THE BASICS

museum.ie

⊞ H8

✉ Kildare Street

☎ 677 7444

🕐 Tue–Sat 10–5, Sun 2–5

🍴 Café

🚊 Pearse

🚌 Cross-city buses; Luas St. Stephen's Green

♿ Good (at ground level)

💷 Free

❓ Shop. Guided tours 45 minutes, small charge

St. Stephen's Green

TOP
25

HIGHLIGHTS

Newman University
Church
● Marble panels
● Carved birds on capitals
● Ceiling
● Golden apse

This oasis of green in the city center was originally common land used for many activities including public hangings. Among notable structures around the green are Newman University Church and Fusiliers' Arch.

A public garden Ireland's famous Victorian public park was reopened in 1880 thanks to the benevolence of Lord Ardilaun, a member of the Guinness family. The park's nine hectares (22 acres) retain the original layout, adorned with an ornamental lake, flowerbeds and crisscrossed with footpaths. Look out for the monuments and public art—everything from a huge statue of a seated Lord Ardilaun to busts of James Joyce. Summer months see free lunchtime concerts in the bandstand.

Clockwise from top left: The Pagoda in St. Stephen's Green; St. Stephen's Green in colorful full bloom in the spring sunshine

Newman University Church Near the entrance to the Green, this ornate, tiny church is Byzantine in style. It was opened in 1856, initially attached to the adjacent Catholic University on land between Nos. 86 and 87, and built by Cardinal Newman to promote his ideals. Inside, the Romanesque porch has four capitals that bear the symbols of evangelistic and angelic figures. Above the main door is a richly decorated arch with an ornamental metal cross.

Fusiliers' Arch This monumental granite gate is also known as Traitors' Arch. It's a tribute to the soldiers of the Royal Dublin Fusiliers killed during the Boer War (1899–1902); the names of those who fell are inscribed on the underside of the arch. On its northeast face are bullet marks thought to be from the 1916 Rising.

THE BASICS

Newman University Church
universitychurch.ie
H8
87A St. Stephen's Green
475 9674
Mon–Sat 8–5, Sun 10–1. Services Mon–Fri at 1pm, Sun at 11am
Cross-city buses; Luas St. Stephen's Green
Pearse
None
Free

Fusiliers' Arch
H8
St. Stephen's Green
Pearse
Cross-city buses; Luas St. Stephen's Green

Trinity College

HIGHLIGHTS

● *Book of Kells*
● *Book of Durrow*
● *Book of Armagh*
● Science Gallery

TIPS

● Everyone wants to see the *Book of Kells* and the best thing is to visit early or come out of season.

● A walking tour in the summer is an informative way to learn more about the college. Ask at the porter's lodge for information.

Stroll around the grounds of the famous college and visit the library, where you will find one of the most joyously decorative manuscripts of the first Christian millennium, the *Book of Kells*.

Surroundings An oasis of fresh air, Trinity College is also the noblest assemblage of classical buildings in the city. Inside, the open square is surrounded on three sides by some of Dublin's finest buildings—Paul Koralek's New Library (1978) to the south, Benjamin Woodward's splendidly carved Museum building (1853–55) to the east and Thomas Burgh's Old Library (1712–32) to the west. In 1857, Woodward altered Burgh's building and made its barrel-vaulted upper floor into a breathtaking space lined with books from floor to ceiling.

Clockwise from top left: Sphere within Sphere (1982–83) by Arnaldo Pomodoro, in the grounds of the college; Trinity College's famous Old Library, housing Ireland's largest collection of books and the Book of Kells; Trinity College, synonymous with learning in Dublin

Book of Kells The library is home to Ireland's greatest collection of medieval manuscripts. Among these, pride of place goes to the *Book of Kells* (c800), a Gospel book that has been bound in four separate sections so that its brilliantly ornamented pages and text may be viewed side by side. Displayed alongside are the important books of *Durrow* (c700) and *Armagh* (c800), the latter giving us most of the information we have about Ireland's patron saint, Patrick. The *Book of Kells* "Turning Darkness into Light" exhibition has excellent displays telling the history of illuminated manuscripts and books. The exit is through the amazing Long Room library.

Science Gallery This gallery stages exhibitions which feature design, discovery and science.

THE BASICS

tcd.ie

🞤 H7

✉ College Green

☎ 896 1000

🕐 Old Library Mon–Sat 9.30–5, Sun 9.30–4.30 (Oct–Apr Sun 12–4.30). Campus daily

🚆 Pearse, Tara Street

🚌 Cross-city buses

♿ Good

💵 Campus free; Library and *Book of Kells* expensive

❓ College tours May–Nov

More to See

DOUGLAS HYDE GALLERY

douglashydegallery.com
Part of the college's site, the
contemporary gallery showcases
talent from Ireland and overseas.
🞢 H7 ✉ Trinity College, Nassau Street
entrance ☎ 608 1116 🕐 Mon–Fri 11–6,
Thu 11–7, Sat 11–4.45 🚋 Pearse 🚌 Cross-
city buses ♿ Few 🎟 Free

GAIETY THEATRE

gaietytheatre.ie
Known as "The Grand Old Lady of
South King Street," this attractive
venue, with its landmark Venetian
facade, opened in 1871 with Sir
Oliver Goldsmith's *She Stoops to
Conquer* followed by burlesque. Its
popular, high-quality entertainment
(▷ 82) continues today.
🞢 H8 ✉ King Street South ☎ 456 9569
🚋 Pearse 🚌 Cross-city buses; Luas
St. Stephen's Green

GRAND CANAL

This pocket of the city has an
atmosphere of calm but is also
home to many of Dublin's most

exciting cultural venues such as the
futuristic Bord Gáis Energy Theatre,
which itself is surrounded by ultramodern apartments. From the
dock here you can take a boat trip
down the canal, or walk along it to
Kilmainham. The Waterways Visitor
Centre traces the story of Ireland's
inland waterways.
🞢 L7 (Grand Canal Docks) 🕐 Visitor
Centre: May–Sep Wed–Sun 10–6; Oct–Apr
Mon–Fri 10–5 🍴 Restaurants and cafés
🚋 Grand Canal Dock 🚌 2, 3

IRISH WHISKEY MUSEUM

irishwhiskeymuseum.ie
Learn about the history of Irish
whiskey with an engaging story-
telling guide, who leads you
through scenes of the distillation
process as far back as Roman
times, with interactive films and
theatrical sets. There's a whiskey
tasting experience at the end.
🞢 H7 ✉ 119 Grafton Street ☎ 525 0970
🕐 Daily 10–6 (last tour 5.30) 🚌 Cross-city
buses; Luas St. Stephen's Green ♿ Good
🎟 Expensive

The square in Grand Canal Dock

IVEAGH GARDENS

iveaghgardens.ie

One of Dublin's finest, yet least-known, parks was designed by Ninian Niven in 1865. The secluded gardens shelter a grotto, fountains, maze, sunken lawns, rockeries, wilderness and woodlands. Exotic tree ferns and pre-1860s rose varieties in the Victorian Rosarium add to the romance of this place.

🕂 H9 ✉ Clonmel Street ☎ 475 7816
🕐 Mon–Sat 8–6, Sun 10–6; closes at dusk in winter 🚌 Cross-city buses; Luas Harcourt
✋ Free

LEINSTER HOUSE

oireachtas.ie

Leinster House is the seat of the Irish government and home to the Dáil Éireann (House of Representatives) and Senead Éireann (Senate). You can visit on a guided tour (Mon–Fri; email to book).

🕂 J8 ✉ Kildare Street ☎ 618 3781
🚉 Pearse 🚌 Cross-city buses; Luas St. Stephen's Green ♿ Good ✋ Free

MERRION SQUARE

Houses surrounding the best-preserved Georgian square in Dublin were home to Daniel O'Connell and William Butler Yeats, among others. The public park is a hidden gem, with well-maintained lawns and a statue of a reclining Oscar Wilde (▷ 76).

🕂 J8 🚉 Pearse 🚌 Cross-city buses ✋ Free

NATIONAL LIBRARY

nli.ie

The library houses the world's largest collection of Irish documentary material, comprising books, newspapers, manuscripts, drawings, maps and photographs. Research has to take place in the reading room. Most popular are the Genealogy Service and family history research departments. There are also excellent exhibitions.

🕂 J7 ✉ Kildare Street ☎ 603 0213
🕐 Mon–Wed 9.30–7.45, Thu–Fri 9.30–4.45, Sat 9.30–12.45 🍴 Café 🚉 Pearse
🚌 Cross-city buses; Luas St. Stephen's Green ♿ Good ✋ Free; reader's ticket required for info

NATIONAL PRINT MUSEUM

nationalprintmuseum.ie

The old chapel houses a collection of thousands of objects related to Ireland's printing industry, with working machinery on display plus printing blocks, photos and books. Guided tours by retired printers bring it to life.

🕂 L9 ✉ Garrison Chapel, Beggar's Bush, Haddington Road ☎ 660 3770 🕐 Mon–Fri 9–5, Sat–Sun 2–5 🚉 Grand Canal Dock
🚌 7, 45, 63 ♿ Good, ground level only
✋ Inexpensive

An elegant door knocker, Merrion Square

NATURAL HISTORY MUSEUM

museum.ie

This museum's old glass cases and creaking floorboards have hardly changed since it was built in 1856. Inside is the skeleton of the giant Irish deer, plus a great array of Irish furred and feathered animals and marine species. The upper floor is given over to animals of the world, including a massive skeleton of a whale suspended majestically from the ceiling.

J8 Merrion Street 677 7444
Tue–Sat 10–5, Sun 2–5 Pearse
Cross-city buses Ground level access only Free

OSCAR WILDE STATUE

Danny Osborne's life-size sculpture of Wilde, at the northwest corner of Merrion Square, was unveiled in 1997 and depicts the writer, lying languidly on a huge piece of granite. It is created from naturally colored Irish stone.

J7 Merrion Square Pearse
Cross-city buses

ST. ANN'S CHURCH

stann.dublin.anglican.org

Patronized by influential residents of Georgian Dublin, this 1720 church has a stunning neo-Romanesque facade. Look for the Bread Shelf, part of a 300-year-old tradition. Organ and choir concerts are held here.

H7 Dawson Street 676 7727
Mon–Fri 10.45–2.45 (11–2 winter) and Sunday service Pearse Cross-city buses Good Free

VIKING SPLASH TOURS

vikingsplash.ie

Drive through Viking Dublin on amphibious buses before driving into the Grand Canal to finish the tour on water. The on-board guide gives an entertaining commentary about the major landmarks along the route. Great fun for kids, who are given Viking helmets to wear.

H8 St. Stephen's Green 707 6000
Feb to mid-Nov regular daily tours depart from St. Stephen's Green (tours last 90 minutes) Expensive

Oscar Wilde statue in Merrion Square

A Viking Splash Tours' land and water vehicle

Georgian
Dublin Walk

Stroll back in time, passing some of the grandest Georgian buildings in Dublin. The squares provide a breath of fresh air in the city.

DISTANCE: 3km (2 miles) **ALLOW:** 2 hours plus stops

START ············

ST. STEPHEN'S GREEN NORTH
(▷ 70–71) ✚ H8 🚍 Cross-city buses

1 Start at the north side of St. Stephen's Green (▷ 70–71), by the famous Shelbourne Hotel (▷ 112), close to Kildare Street. Walk down this street.

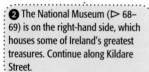

2 The National Museum (▷ 68–69) is on the right-hand side, which houses some of Ireland's greatest treasures. Continue along Kildare Street.

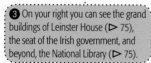

3 On your right you can see the grand buildings of Leinster House (▷ 75), the seat of the Irish government, and beyond, the National Library (▷ 75).

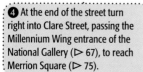

4 At the end of the street turn right into Clare Street, passing the Millennium Wing entrance of the National Gallery (▷ 67), to reach Merrion Square (▷ 75).

············ **END**

ST. STEPHEN'S GREEN SOUTH
(▷ 70–71) ✚ H8 🚍 Cross-city buses

8 At the end of the street turn right onto Leeson Street Lower, and keep going until you reach the south edge of St. Stephen's Green.

7 Continue onto Fitzwilliam Street Upper to Fitzwilliam Square, and turn right along its southern edge. Some of the best Georgian houses are here—take a note of the doors and fanlights above. Turn left at the end of the square onto Pembroke Street Upper.

6 Walk along Merrion Square West and left into Merrion Square South. At the end is Number Twenty Nine, a gracious Georgian town house and museum (currently closed for major renovation). Turn right here.

5 Turn right here—across the road at No. 1, is Oscar Wilde's House.

Shopping

ALIAS TOM

aliastom.com

One of Dublin's longest-standing men's stores, now with womenswear, stocks top labels including Armani, René Lezard and Paul Smith.

 H7 🖂 Duke Lane ☎ 671 5443
🚆 Pearse 🚌 Cross-city buses

ARAN SWEATER MARKET

aransweatermarket.com

Specialists in Aran sweaters since 1892, made in the tiny island community of Inis More, the woolens here are top quality. There is a wide selection—everything from chunky men's sweaters to women's pretty ponchos and coats. Look out for the vintage photos on the stairwell's walls.

H7 🖂 Lower Grafton Street ☎ 888 3606
🚌 Cross-city buses

AVOCA

avoca.ie

This is one of Ireland's oldest surviving businesses. Founded in 1723 and developed as a fine department store, it has unique and exclusive high-quality items combining the traditional with the fashionable. The splendid food hall is packed with Irish delicacies including preserves, oils and biscuits, all under the Avoca label. There's also a lovely café.

H7 🖂 11–13 Suffolk Street ☎ 677 4215
🚆 Pearse 🚌 Cross-city buses

BROWN THOMAS

brownthomas.com

Ireland's stylish department store showcases Irish and international designer clothes. Also you will find household furnishings, cosmetics, leather goods, accessories and linens. Level 2 is home to BT2, with casual fashions from well-known designers.

H7 🖂 88–95 Grafton Street ☎ 605 6666
🚆 Pearse 🚌 Cross-city buses

BUTLER'S CHOCOLATE CAFÉ

butlerschocolates.com

Mouth-watering selection of Irish hand-made chocolates from the original Mrs Bailey-Butler's recipe of 1932.

H7 🖂 51A Grafton Street ☎ 616 7004
🚆 Pearse 🚌 Cross-city buses

CELTIC WHISKEY SHOP

celticwhiskeyshop.com

A tempting selection of whiskeys from Ireland and around the world—one of the city's best ranges—plus, chocolates, liqueurs and wines.

H7 🖂 27–28 Dawson Street ☎ 675 9744
🚆 Pearse 🚌 Cross-city buses

CHARLES BYRNE

charlesbyrne.com

Established in 1870, Charles Byrne is renowned for its expertise in stringed instruments, from mandolins to cellos. It also stocks Ireland's best range of *bodhráns* (traditional Gaelic drums), which are all handmade by experts.

G7 🖂 21–22 Lower Stephen Street
☎ 478 1773 🚆 Pearse 🚌 Cross-city buses

MADE IN IRELAND

If you're looking for something of modern Ireland for your home, check out the following:

● Jerpoint Glass—heavy, hand-blown pieces of simple design with color bursts.
● Waterford Crystal—John Rocha's minimalist designer line has brought Waterford crystal bang up-to-date.
● Ceramics—look out for Nicholas Mosse's pottery and great designs by Louis Mulcahy, one of Ireland's most prolific ceramicists.

CLEO

cleo-ltd.com

If hand-knit sweaters, tweedy skirts and high-end country style is your preference, then Cleo's is the place for you. Run by the Joyce family since 1936, Cleo's specializes in natural-fiber clothes made in the knitters' and weavers' own homes.

H8 ✉ 18 Kildare Street ☎ 676 1421 🚉 Pearse 🚌 Cross-city buses

DESIGNYARD

designyard.ie

This venue for crafts and decorative arts has a stunning jewelry gallery showcasing pieces by Irish designers. Jewelry here is made with both precious and non-precious materials and there are lovely glass and ceramics pieces too.

H7 ✉ 25 South Frederick Street ☎ 474 1011 🚉 Pearse 🚌 Cross-city buses

DUBRAY BOOKS

dubraybooks.ie

One of Dublin's independent booksellers, Dubray Books stocks an extensive collection of titles, including fiction, children's favorites, biographies and a large section on Irish history, fiction and biographies.

H7 ✉ 36 Grafton Street ☎ 677 5568 🚌 Cross-city buses; Luas St. Stephen's Green

GALLERY 29

gallery29.ie

The Irish-owned store is the place to come for vintage posters. Here you'll find examples from the 1890s to 1990s, mainly advertising posters for food, travel and arts—all of them original. They can also mount and frame them for you.

H7 ✉ 29 Molesworth Street ☎ 642 5784 🚉 Pearse 🚌 Cross-city buses

HODGES FIGGIS

waterstones.com/bookshops/hodges-figgis

Spread over an impressive four floors, this famous old bookstore was established in 1768 and is particularly revered for its extensive collection of works on Celtic and Irish history, culture, art and literature.

H7 ✉ 56–58 Dawson Street ☎ 677 4754 🚉 Pearse 🚌 Cross-city buses

HOUSE OF IRELAND

houseofireland.com

Traditional Irish fashion, crafts, Waterford Crystal, Belleek china and Aran knitwear. Also the less well-known, attractive Galway Crystal can be found here.

H7 ✉ 38 Nassau Street ☎ 671 1111 🚉 Pearse 🚌 Cross-city buses

JAMES FOX

jamesfox.ie

Established in 1881, this family-run specialist cigar and whiskey store stocks Ireland's largest selection of handmade Cuban cigars, complete with official Habanos certificates of authenticity. It's also a great place to find rare Irish single malt whiskeys.

H7 ✉ 119 Grafton Street ☎ 677 0533 🚌 Cross-city buses; Luas St. Stephen's Green

WHAT'S YOUR STYLE?

There are some great shops in Dublin displaying a wide range of home interior products, many produced by Irish crafts-people and also by fashion designers turning to objects and furniture. Interior design is popular worldwide, and Dublin is gaining more shops for the enthusiast. Beautiful items in stone, wood, glass and other natural materials can be bought in both traditional and contemporary styles. You'll find items by Terence Conran, John Rocha and other well-known names.

JOHNSON'S COURT

An upmarket collection of top-notch jewelry shops nestled in a small alley-way. Choose from a range of goods, from luxury watches at Paul Sheeran to wedding rings at Donovan & Matson.
H7 Off Grafton Street Cross-city buses; Luas St. Stephen's Green

JORGENSEN GALLERY

jorgensenfineart.com
Ireland's most popular fashion designer, Ib Jorgensen, turned to fine art in 1992 and hasn't looked back. Prepare to pay top prices for 19th- and 20th-century artists such as Ken Moroney, Maria Levinge and Kevin Gaines, and works by Mark Rode, Cody Swanson and Mary Swanzy. Also solo exhibitions of international contemporary artists.
H7 35 Molesworth Street 661 9721
Pearse Cross-city buses

KERLIN GALLERY

kerlingallery.com
This is one of Dublin's leading contem-porary art galleries, established in 1988, showcasing the work of top artists like Dorothy Cross, Aleana Egan, David Godbold and Sean Scully.

H7 Anne's Lane, off South Anne Street
670 9093 Pearse Cross-city buses

KEVIN AND HOWLIN

kevinandhowlin.com
Shop here for your hand-woven Donegal tweeds, made exclusively for the store. All the usual hardwearing items—jackets, waistcoats, hats and ties, in both modern and traditional styles—are of the highest quality.
H7 31 Nassau Street 633 4576
Pearse Cross-city buses

KILKENNY

kilkennyshop.com
This large emporium sells stylish Irish decorative objects such as Waterford Crystal, books, fashion and Celtic-inspired jewelry, with pieces from designers such as Orla Kiely. Great café-restaurant over-looking Trinity College's grounds.
H7 6–15 Nassau Street 677 7066
Pearse Cross-city buses

LOUISE KENNEDY

louisekennedy.com
Kennedy's tasteful, exclusive clothing and crystal collections are sold alongside luxury branded accessories and gifts.
J8 56 Merrion Square 662 0056
Pearse Cross-city buses

MAGILLS

Salami, meats, bread, cheese, coffee, herbs, spices and every sort of savory delicacy are crammed into this fabulous and atmospheric deli.
H7 14 Clarendon Street 671 3830
Pearse Cross-city buses

ST. STEPHEN'S GREEN CENTRE

stephensgreen.com
A light, airy mall over three floors com-bines more expensive specialist shops

with Dunnes department store, bargain emporia and a food court.

⊞ H8 ✉ Corner of Grafton Street and St. Stephen's Green ☎ 478 0888 🚆 Pearse 🚌 Cross-city bus

SECRET BOOK & RECORD STORE

Tucked away, this much-loved Dublin gem sells second-hand paperbacks, classic novels, modern art books and even records.

⊞ H7 ✉ 15a Wicklow Street ☎ 679 7272 🚌 Cross-city buses; Luas St. Stephen's Green

SHERIDANS CHEESE SHOP

sheridanscheesemongers.com

This glorious shop packed with blocks of cheese is a wonderful showcase for Irish farmhouse varieties that are now winning awards worldwide. It also sells a range of Irish foods such as salmon and marmalades.

⊞ H8 ✉ 11 South Anne Street ☎ 679 3143 🚆 Pearse 🚌 Cross-city buses

SILVER SHOP

silvershopdublin.com

Have a browse here and admire the wide range of antique silver and silver-plate, from the conventional to the unusual Irish portrait miniatures. Prices

IRELAND'S INTERNATIONAL DESIGNERS

Dublin fashion stores carry a great mix of contemporary, alternative and classic collections. Irish designers to look for include John Rocha, Paul Costelloe, Lainey Keogh, Daryl Kerrigan and Philip Treacy. Check out the handbags by Helen Cody and Orla Kiely, Vivienne Walsh's intricate jewelry, Pauric Sweeney's witty postmodern accessories stocked at Hobo and Slim Barrett's quirky fairy-tale tiaras.

start low and head way up into the thousands of euros.

⊞ H7 ✉ 59 South William Street ☎ 679 4147 🚆 Pearse 🚌 Cross-city buses

STOCK DESIGN

Come to this exciting store for house wares including furniture, fabrics, rugs, lighting and an impressive range of fun and functional kitchen utensils and cookware. Serious cooks will come across more unusual items and some one-off accessories.

⊞ H8 ✉ 33–34 King Street South ☎ 679 4316 🚆 Pearse 🚌 Cross-city buses

TRINITY SWEATERS

sweatershop.com

The knitted Aran sweaters, Merino-wool ponchos, cashmere capes and Celtic scarves would make a great addition to anyone's wardrobe.

⊞ H7 ✉ 30 Nassau Street ☎ 671 2292 🚌 Cross-city buses; Luas St. Stephen's Green

ULYSSES RARE BOOKS

rarebooks.ie

Formerly known as Cathach Books, this is Dublin's leading rare and antiquarian bookshop, specializing in books of Irish interest, with a particular emphasis on 20th-century literature.

⊞ H7 ✉ 10 Duke Street ☎ 671 8676 🚆 Pearse 🚌 Cross-city buses

WEIR & SONS

weirandsons.ie

Founded in 1869, this family-run jewelry business is one of Grafton Street's most established shops. Look for top brands, including antique silver and luxury watches, and be looked after by the exquisite service.

⊞ H7 ✉ 96–99 Grafton Street ☎ 677 9678 🚌 Cross-city buses; Luas St. Stephen's Green

Entertainment and Nightlife

BLEEDING HORSE

bleedinghorse.ie

A long-established bar, with a history dating back to 1649, the Bleeding Horse covers several levels. It's popular with locals and students—the latter of which fill it especially at weekends when there is live music.

➕ G9 ✉ 24–25 Upper Camden Street ☎ 475 2705 🚌 Cross-city buses; Luas Harcourt

BRUXELLES

bruxelles.ie

Three bars in one, tucked away off Grafton Street, are best known for their live rock bands, plus regular DJ nights. There's a big screen showing major sports events, and a convivial saloon bar with a proud music heritage. There's a huge statue of Irish singer and song-writer Phil Lynott outside.

➕ H7 ✉ 7 Harry Street ☎ 677 5362 🚌 Cross-city buses; Luas St. Stephen's Green

CAFÉ EN SEINE

cafeenseine.ie

The beautiful interior of this long bar has strikingly high ceilings supporting French bistro lighting. The relaxed daytime atmosphere hots up in the evening and lines form after 11pm on weekends.

➕ H7 ✉ 39 Dawson Street ☎ 677 4567 🚇 Pearse 🚌 Cross-city buses

RAISING A GLASS

The Irish have a reputation for enjoying a tipple and it's not surprising given the quality of their native drinks. For stout sample Guinness or Murphy's. For whiskey—a traditional chaser to your stout—there's Jamesons or Bushmills. And don't forget Baileys, made from two of Ireland's finest products—whiskey and cream.

DOHENY AND NESBITT

dohenyandnesbitt.ie

A distinguished old pub, Doheny and Nesbitt attracts politicians and media people, as well as tourists and locals, to its three floors and welcoming bars that are well-stocked with whiskeys and stouts. Victorian-style mirrored walls, high ceilings and intimate snugs reflect its 19th-century origins. There's also a special Whiskey Corner.

➕ J8 ✉ 5 Lower Baggot Street ☎ 676 2945 🚌 10, 15X, 25X, 49X

GAIETY THEATRE

gaietytheatre.ie

An integral part of Dublin theaterland, this longstanding venue stages opera, musicals, classic plays, comedies, pantomime and touring shows. The Gaiety's agenda is ambitious. Stop by to hear lunchtime arias during the opera season.

➕ H8 ✉ King Street South ☎ 456 9569 🚇 Pearse 🚌 Cross-city buses

THE HORSESHOE BAR

shelbournedining.ie

Over the decades, many a famous face has come to sit in the bar of the grand Shelbourne Hotel (▷ 112) to enjoy a drink. Try a Dublin classic, a Black Velvet cocktail, made from Champagne and Guinness, and said to have been created here.

➕ H8 ✉ The Shelbourne Dublin, 27 St. Stephen's Green ☎ 663 4500 🚌 Cross-city buses; Luas St. Stephen's Green

INTERNATIONAL BAR

international-bar.com

Indulge in a hefty helping of Irish wit at the home of the Comedy Cellar, founded by Irish comic geniuses Ardal O'Hanlon, Dylan Moran and many

others. The daily evening schedule of events includes stand-up and improv comedy, plus poetry, spoken word recitals and jazz.

🔳 H7 ✉ 23 Wicklow Street ☎ 677 9250
🚇 Pearse 🚌 Cross-city buses

KENNEDY'S
kennedyspub.ie

The basement club in this building, Kennedy's Station, is home to DJs on weekends with a very different vibe, yet the regular bar manages to retain its traditional and old-world charm. Due to its close proximity to Trinity College, it is popular with students. There's also a restaurant upstairs.

🔳 J7 ✉ 31–32 Westland Row ☎ 679 9077
🚇 Pearse 🚌 Cross-city buses

LILLIE'S BORDELLO
lilliesbordello.ie

This celebrity-rich cocktail lounge and bar is all about low lighting, deep red sofas and opulent decor. It's mainly members only, but if you dress well you may get entry. Music is mainly house, garage, chart R&B and funk but the playlist also includes a healthy dose of mainstream pop and club classics.

🔳 H7 ✉ Adam Court, Grafton Street ☎ 679 9204 🚇 Pearse 🚌 Cross-city buses

MULLIGANS
mulligans.ie

A pub since 1820, Mulligans is a Guinness drinker's institution and has a long association with journalists and the Theatre Royal, opposite, and can boast many famous visitors including James Joyce and even President J.F. Kennedy. Retaining its Victorian mahogany furnishings, it has resisted change.

🔳 H6 ✉ 8 Poolbeg Street ☎ 677 5582
🚇 Tara Street 🚌 Cross-city buses

THE CLASSICS

Dublin has a thriving classical music and opera scene, though performances are irregular. The National Concert Hall stages a full schedule but other venues offer seasonal performances only. The Gaiety Theatre plays host to Dublin's most professional and prolific opera society. To find out about forthcoming events, call the box offices direct or check the listings in the *Irish Times*. Reservations are recommended for most of the performances.

NATIONAL CONCERT HALL
nch.ie

This busy Georgian concert hall with a modern 250-seat auditorium and world-class acoustics is home to the RTÉ National Symphony Orchestra and other Irish ensembles. Top artists perform here. A recent major redevelopment of the concert hall resulted in a new recital room, plus a new atrium winter garden café.

🔳 H9 ✉ Earlsfort Terrace ☎ 417 0000
🚇 Pearse 🚌 14, 14A, 15A, 44, 74

O'DONOGHUE'S
odonoghues.ie

Renowned for its associations with the famous Irish folk group the Dubliners, O'Donoghue's is a good place for nightly impromptu sessions of traditional music but it does get crowded.

🔳 J8 ✉ 15 Merrion Row ☎ 660 7194
🚇 Pearse 🚌 Cross-city buses

PERUKE & PERIWIG
peruke.ie

In a former wig-making store (hence the name), this cocktail bar harks back to 19th-century decadence, complete with dark mahogany and plush velvet decor. This is a full bar with a whiskey

menu, but it's the cocktails that really are the appeal, complete with hand-made fruit syrups and unique recipes. It also serves dinner.

🔡 H8 ✉ 31 Dawson Street ☎ 672 7190 🚌 Cross-city buses; Luas St. Stephen's Green

POD
pod.ie

The Place of Dance is one of the most popular clubs in town. It's a different club each evening with a good mix of happy house and popular dance floor hits. Try the Lobby Bar for a drink before hitting Crawdaddy or Tripod clubs, all on the same premises.

🔡 G9 ✉ Old Harcourt Station, 35 Harcourt Street ☎ 4776 3374 🚌 Cross-city buses; Luas Harcourt

THE SCHOOLHOUSE BAR
schoolhousehotel.com

Set in a lovely hotel with a small garden (▷ 111), this bar is in the fashionable Ballsbridge neighborhood. The building, a converted school, keeps many of its original features. Food is served all day, and there is live music Thursday through to Saturday.

🔡 K8 ✉ 2–8 Northumberland Road ☎ 667 5014 🚌 Grand Canal Dock

THE SUGAR CLUB
thesugarclub.com

In a converted cinema, this multipurpose arts center has regular live bands, DJ nights and occasional film screenings.

🔡 H9 ✉ 8 Lower Leeson Street ☎ 678 7188 🚉 Pearse 🚌 10, 11, 14, 15, 44, 46, 86

Where to Eat

<table>
<tr><th colspan="2">PRICES</th></tr>
<tr><td colspan="2">Prices are approximate, based on a 3-course meal for one person.</td></tr>
<tr><td>€€€</td><td>over €50</td></tr>
<tr><td>€€</td><td>€30–€50</td></tr>
<tr><td>€</td><td>under €30</td></tr>
</table>

3FE (€)
3fe.com

One of a new breed of cool cafés in Dublin, this one boasts top roasts in a relaxed, rustic environment where you can get breakfast, brunch or lunch. You can even join a class (fee) to learn the best way to brew coffee.

🔡 K8 ✉ 32 Grand Canal Street ☎ No phone 🕐 Mon 8–5, Sat–Sun 9–6 🚉 Grand Canal Dock 🚌 Cross-city buses

BANG RESTAURANT (€€–€€€)
bangrestaurant.com

Cool and minimal, Bang attracts an energetic clientele, and its eclectic, modern European menu matches its chic interiors. It offers a five-course tasting menu.

🔡 J8 ✉ 11 Merrion Row ☎ 400 4229 🕐 Lunch, dinner Mon–Sat 🚉 Pearse 🚌 Cross-city buses

BEWLEY'S CAFÉ (€)
bewleys.com

Steeped in tradition and nostalgia, Bewley's has been here since 1840. Reopening after major refurbishment in 2017, it's operating on only the ground level, rather than its previous three floors. This flagship branch of the

famous Bewley's chain promises to remain an iconic venue, with fairtrade coffee and a simple daytime menu.
🔲 H7 ✉ 78 Grafton Street ☎ 672 7720
🕐 Mon–Wed 8am–10pm, Thu–Sat 8am–11pm, Sun 9am–10pm 🚉 Pearse 🚌 Cross-city buses

CHILI CLUB (€€)
chiliclub.ie
This tiny, simple restaurant is loved for its fiery Thai curries, plus fresh stir-fried shrimp in ginger, pad Thai and tangy Thai soups.
🔲 H7 ✉ 1 Anne's Lane, off Anne Street South ☎ 677 3721 🕐 Lunch Mon–Fri, dinner daily 🚉 Pearse 🚌 Cross-city buses

CORNUCOPIA (€)
cornucopia.ie
Wholefood and vegetarian dishes are served in a sunny dining room. Home-made dishes from breakfast through to dinner, with fresh salads, hot stews and delicious cakes; plus vegan dishes.
🔲 H7 ✉ 19 Wicklow Street ☎ 677 7583
🕐 Breakfast, lunch and dinner Mon–Sat (Sun 12–9) 🚉 Pearse 🚌 Cross-city buses

DAX (€€€)
dax.ie
This renowned Irish-French restaurant serves food in an intimate basement in a Georgian building. Its ever-changing seven-course menu may include Wicklow venison loin in red wine jus and sea bream with braised seaweed.
🔲 J9 ✉ 23 Pembroke Street Upper ☎ 676 1494 🕐 Lunch Tue–Fri, dinner Tue–Sat
🚌 11, 11A, 46; Luas Harcourt

DIEP LE SHAKER (€€–€€€)
diep.net
Established nearly 20 years ago, this family-run business is as popular today

as it was when it first opened. A stylish haunt, the restaurant offers very tasty, authentic and well-presented Thai cuisine, made using Irish meats.
🔲 J8 ✉ 55 Pembroke Lane ☎ 661 1829
🕐 Lunch Tue–Fri, dinner Tue–Sat
🚉 Lansdowne Road 🚌 Cross-city buses

DUNNE & CRESCENZI (€€)
dunneandcrescenzi.com
This authentic Italian bistro has an extensive menu of specialties including slow-cooked Tuscan sausage. Enjoy the relaxed atmosphere, well-prepared food made with quality ingredients, and good Italian wines.
🔲 H7 ✉ 14–16 South Frederick Street
☎ 675 9892 🕐 All-day dining 🚉 Pearse
🚌 Cross-city buses

L'ECRIVAIN (€€€)
lecrivain.com
Chef Derry Clarke's popular Michelin-starred Modern Irish restaurant continues to grow in stature. It is well known for its fresh fish, caught off the Irish coast, and its organic Irish meat.
🔲 J8 ✉ 109a Lower Baggot Street
☎ 661 1919 🕐 Lunch Mon–Fri, dinner Mon–Sat 🚌 10

TIPS FOR EATING OUT

● Eating out is very popular in Dublin, so reserve ahead. Some restaurants close on Monday. Most upscale restaurants offer an excellent-value fixed-price lunch menu.
● Pre-theater or early-bird set menus are popular, a value meal usually served before 7pm.
● A service charge of 12.5 per cent may be added to your bill, especially if a group of people are dining. If service is not included, a sum of 12.5–15 per cent is the usual added tip.

THE SOUTHEAST WHERE TO EAT

THE FARM (€€)

thefarmfood.ie

With outside seating, great for people-watching, this restaurant serves healthy, organic Irish products. Farm charcuterie, home-smoked duck breast and Irish fish pie are some of the dishes on its regularly changing menu. Good vegetarian selection.

➕ H7 ✉ 3 Dawson Street ☎ 671 8654 🕐 Lunch and dinner daily 🚌 Cross-city buses; Luas St. Stephen's Green

FIRE (€€€)

mansionhouse.ie

The spacious dining room is set in the resplendent belle époque era in the Mansion House, built in 1715 to house the Mayor of Dublin. It offers a modern European menu with a twist. Jumbo tiger prawns from the wood-fired oven and prime steaks are the signature dishes. Pre-theater meals are good value.

➕ H8 ✉ The Mansion House, Dawson Street ☎ 676 7200 🕐 Dinner daily 🚌 Cross-city buses

THE GOTHAM CAFÉ (€–€€)

gothamcafe.ie

Lively, family-friendly café-restaurant famed for its pizzas. Enjoy imaginative

---

PUB GRUB

Pubs in Dublin are synonymous with drinking, Guinness, traditional Irish music and good *craic*. But pub food is popular and, particularly for those on a limited budget, good value. You can get some excellent hearty meals, including traditional Irish stews, the boxty (potato pancake) and colcannon (cabbage and potato). There is often a carvery offering a choice of salads. Sample any of these accompanied by a pint of Guinness to be like a local.

---

toppings, plus pasta and vegetarian dishes, huge salads and a kids' menu. Its walls are adorned with covers of *Rolling Stone* magazine.

➕ H7 ✉ 8 Anne Street South ☎ 679 5266 🕐 Lunch and dinner daily 🚌 Cross-city buses; Luas St. Stephen's Green

THE GREENHOUSE (€€€)

thegreenhouserestaurant.ie

This relatively new dining establishment, already with a Michelin star, is sophistication without pretension. With an interesting menu of contemporary European cuisine, enjoy its five or six-course "surprise tasting menu," showing off the Finnish chef Viljanen's exciting and inventive dishes.

➕ H8 ✉ Dawson Street, off St. Stephen's Green ☎ 676 7015 🕐 Lunch and dinner Tue–Sat 🚌 Cross-city buses; Luas St. Stephen's Green

HATCH & SONS IRISH KITCHEN (€–€€)

hatchandsons.co

A welcoming café-restaurant inside the interesting Little Museum of Dublin (▷ 66), which celebrates fresh Irish ingredients. Traditional dishes on the menu include beef and Guinness stew, smoked fish platters and fresh sandwiches. A few craft beers make a good accompaniment.

➕ H8 ✉ 15 St. Stephen's Green ☎ 661 0075 🕐 Breakfast, lunch and early evening daily 🚌 Cross-city buses; Luas St. Stephen's Green

LANGKAWI (€€)

langkawi.ie

Excellent Malaysian restaurant with an exciting, extensive menu reflecting the influences of Chinese, Indian and Malay cuisine. Specialties include spicy *kapitan*

and *gulai* curries, with seafood, meat and vegetarian dishes.

➕ K9 ✉ 46 Upper Baggot Street ☎ 668 2760 🕐 Lunch Mon–Fri, dinner daily 🚇 Lansdowne Road 🚌 10

MAO (€–€€)

mymao.ie

Enjoy fresh, authentic Thai, Malaysian and Indonesian dishes in contemporary surroundings. Specialties include *nasi goreng* and five spice chicken.

➕ H7 ✉ 2 Chatham Row ☎ 670 4899 🕐 Lunch and dinner daily 🚇 Pearse 🚌 Cross-city buses

MARCO PIERRE WHITE STEAKHOUSE & GRILL (€€€)

marcopierrewhite.ie

This excellent restaurant specializes in quality Irish beef, in ribeye, sirloin and fillet, with a choice of classic sauces. Seafood dishes include yellow fin tuna steaks. Good-value early-bird menu.

➕ H8 ✉ 51 Dawson Street ☎ 677 1155 🕐 Lunch and dinner daily 🚇 Pearse 🚌 Cross-city buses

OSTERIA LUCIO (€€)

osterialucio.com

In the new IT hub around the Grand Canal; this contemporary Italian restaurant is all about industrial chic, wooden tables and exposed brick walls, tucked in a tunnel under a railway bridge. The exquisite cuisine is all about finesse, with beautifully presented dishes.

➕ K8 ✉ The Malting Tower, Clanwilliam Terrace ☎ 6624 199 🕐 Lunch and dinner Mon–Sat 🚇 Pearse 🚌 Cross-city buses

PEARL BRASSERIE (€€€)

pearl-brasserie.com

Classy restaurant with romantic alcoves, an oyster bar, modern art on the walls

EARLY START

The traditional Irish breakfast consists of bacon, sausage, egg, mushrooms, tomato, black-and-white pudding (a sausage-shaped meat product made from cows' blood and served in fried slices) and toast, washed down with strong tea or coffee. But few working Dubliners have time to indulge, except perhaps on weekends. Led by the power breakfast business community, ever more city dwellers are beginning to eat out first thing in the morning.

and an inventive menu that includes local fish and game dishes. A real treat.

➕ J8 ✉ 20 Merrion Street Upper ☎ 661 3572 🕐 Lunch and dinner Mon–Sat 🚇 Pearse 🚌 Cross-city buses

LA PENICHE (€€)

lapeniche.ie

La Peniche is on a barge which cruises the Dublin Canal, or may stay moored up. Either way it's a good alternative eating venue. The food is French/Italian bistro style; simple but local and organic produce is used with excellent results. Fully licensed, serving French wines, beers and ciders.

➕ J9 ✉ Grand Canal, Mespil Road ☎ 087 790 0077 (mobile) 🕐 Dinner Wed–Sun 🚇 Grand Canal Dock 🚌 10, 10A, 18

THE PIG'S EAR (€€)

thepigsear.ie

This upstairs restaurant overlooks Trinity College. The renowned Irish chef, Stephen McAllister, cooks contemporary Irish food. It's an informal restaurant offering good-value lunch and early evening set menus.

➕ H7 ✉ 4 Nassau Street ☎ 670 3865 🕐 Lunch and dinner Mon–Sat 🚇 Pearse 🚌 Cross-city buses

RESTAURANT PATRICK GUILBAUD (€€€)

restaurantpatrickguilbaud.ie

Superlative fine dining by French chef Guillaume Lebrun, with dishes of blue lobster and Wicklow lamb, and desserts to die for. A tastefully decorated restaurant and a lovely collection of Irish art.

🖽 J8 ⊠ 21 Upper Merrion Street ☎ 676 4192 🕐 Lunch and dinner Tue–Sat 🚊 Pearse 🚌 Cross-city buses

SABA (€€)

sabadublin.com

Serving first-class Thai and Vietnamese food using organic and Fairtrade ingredients, the setting at Saba (meaning "happy meeting place") is stylish.

🖽 H7 ⊠ 26–28 Clarendon Street ☎ 679 2000 🕐 Lunch and dinner daily 🚊 Pearse 🚌 Cross-city buses

THE SADDLE ROOM (€€€)

marriott.co.uk

The refurbished Shelbourne Hotel (▷ 112) has produced a smart, contemporary steak and seafood restaurant. The Oyster Bar, with its comfy leather banquettes and intimate setting, is one side of the opulent fine dining room. High-quality, locally sourced ingredients produce dishes such as confit duck leg, roast venison and roast turbot.

🖽 H8 ⊠ 27 St. Stephen's Green ☎ 663 4500 🕐 Breakfast, lunch and dinner daily 🚊 Pearse 🚌 Cross-city buses

SCIENCE GALLERY CAFÉ (€)

dublin.sciencegallery.com

This bright and breezy casual café lies inside the glass-and-steel Science Gallery at Trinity College. It offers breakfast, hot sandwiches and stone-baked pizza, plus a bar.

🖽 J7 ⊠ Trinity College, Pearse Street

☎ 896 4091 🕐 Breakfast, lunch and early evening Mon–Fri, Sat–Sun from noon 🚊 Pearse 🚌 Cross-city buses

SHANAHAN'S ON THE GREEN (€€€)

shanahans.ie

A highly regarded American steak and seafood restaurant, Shanahan's is located in an elegant Georgian house. Enjoy top cuts of mature Angus steak, and choose from one of the 5,000 wines from the extensive cellar. Excellent service.

🖽 H8 ⊠ 119 St. Stephen's Green ☎ 407 0939 🕐 Lunch Friday; dinner Mon–Sat (Sun also in summer) 🚌 Cross-city buses; Luas St. Stephen's Green

THE UNICORN RESTAURANT (€€–€€€)

theunicorn.restaurant

Understated elegance is the key to this classic Italian restaurant, established in 1938, in a quiet courtyard. It's all about smart white tablecloths and a candlelit interior, with a select menu of *primi* and *secondi*, with meat and fish dishes. There is an excellent wine selection.

🖽 J8 ⊠ 12b Merrion Court ☎ 662 4757 🕐 Lunch and dinner Mon–Sat 🚊 Pearse 🚌 Cross-city buses

WILD RESTAURANT (€€)

doylecollection.com

Located in the Westbury Hotel (▷ 112), this is the perfect place for afternoon tea with great views of Grafton Street. Its regular menu has international dishes from seasonal Irish ingredients.

🖽 H7 ⊠ Grafton Street ☎ 646 3352 🕐 Lunch and dinner daily (last meal orders 9.30pm Sun–Mon); afternoon tea 3pm–5.30pm 🚊 Pearse 🚌 Cross-city buses

Farther Afield

Just a short distance outside Dublin the beautiful Irish countryside is a delight, with pretty seaside villages, stunning lakes and ancient Celtic burial sites. A trip to the suburbs can also be rewarding.

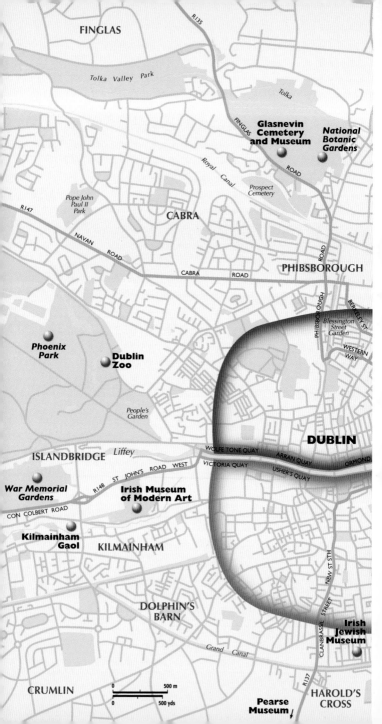

FINGLAS

R135

Tolka Valley Park

Tolka

FINGLAS

Glasnevin Cemetery and Museum

National Botanic Gardens

ROAD

Royal Canal

Prospect Cemetery

R147

Pope John Paul II Park

CABRA

NAVAN ROAD

CABRA ROAD

ROAD

PHIBSBOROUGH

PHIBSBOROUGH

BERKELEY ST

Blessington Street Garden

WESTERN WAY

Phoenix Park

Dublin Zoo

People's Garden

Liffey

DUBLIN

WOLFE TONE QUAY

ARRAN QUAY

ORMOND

ISLANDBRIDGE

VICTORIA QUAY

USHER'S QUAY

War Memorial Gardens

R148   ST JOHN'S ROAD WEST

Irish Museum of Modern Art

CON COLBERT ROAD

Kilmainham Gaol

KILMAINHAM

DOLPHIN'S BARN

NEW ST STH

CLANBRASSIL STREET

Irish Jewish Museum

Grand Canal

CRUMLIN

0   500 m

0   500 yds

R137

Pearse Museum

HAROLD'S CROSS

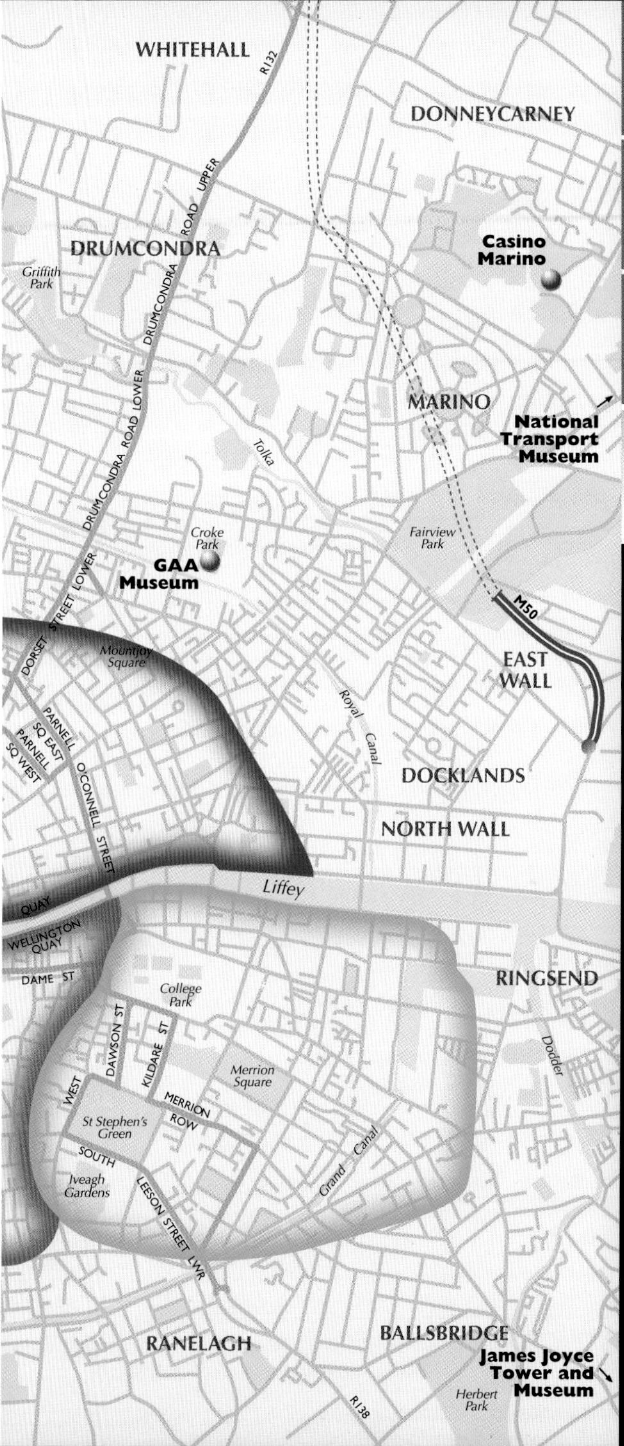

WHITEHALL

R132

DONNEYCARNEY

DRUMCONDRA

Griffith Park

Casino Marino

DRUMCONDRA ROAD UPPER

MARINO

National Transport Museum

Tolka

DRUMCONDRA ROAD LOWER

Fairview Park

Croke Park

GAA Museum

Mountjoy Square

M50

EAST WALL

DORSET STREET LOWER

PARNELL SQ EAST

PARNELL SQ WEST

O'CONNELL STREET

Royal Canal

DOCKLANDS

NORTH WALL

QUAY

WELLINGTON QUAY

Liffey

DAME ST

RINGSEND

College Park

WEST

DAWSON ST

KILDARE ST

Merrion Square

Dodder

MERRION ROW

St Stephen's Green

SOUTH

Iveagh Gardens

LEESON STREET LWR

Grand Canal

RANELAGH

BALLSBRIDGE

James Joyce Tower and Museum

Herbert Park

R138

Dublin Zoo

The Kaziranga Forest Trail is home to the zoo's elephants (left); an African (western lowland) gorilla (right)

THE BASICS

dublinzoo.ie

🚼 B5

✉ Phoenix Park

☎ 474 8900

🕐 Mar–Sep daily 9.30–6; Oct 9.30–5.30; Nov–Dec 9.30–4; Jan 9.30–4.30; Feb 9.30–5. Last admission 1 hour before closing

🚌 10, 10A, 25, 26, 66, 66A, 66B, 67, 67A; Luas Heuston

🍴 Restaurant, cafés

♿ Good

💷 Expensive

HIGHLIGHTS

● African Savanna
● Gorilla Rainforest
● Lions and tigers in the Asian Forests
● Family Farm

Opened in 1831, this is one of the world's oldest public zoos. Today, within its 24ha (60 acres) of space inside Phoenix Park, it is home to more than 700 animals from around the globe.

Zoo's residents The zoo is set out with easy-to-navigate walkways, with two large lakes spreading down the center. There are a variety of habitats, re-creating the natural habitats of the animals as closely as is possible in chilly Ireland. The Gorilla Rainforest, for example, is home to seven huge western lowland gorillas who have views of the surrounds from their trees and rocky outcrops. There is also a breeding program here. Giraffes and zebras prowl the African Savanna, which they share with rhino, oryx and ostrich. Fans of big cats will head to the Asian Forests, inspired by India's Gir Forest. Here you can see the lion habitat, which is a close reflection of their natural environment and encourages natural behavior. Huge blocks of Donegal sandstone and many tons of sand form the Penguin Habitat, where you can watch a dozen Humboldt penguins frolicking.

Family attractions Younger kids will love the Family Farm, where they can mingle with the smaller, and safer, animals in a space that re-creates a typical Irish farm with sheep, goats, cows and pigs. Events include milking demonstrations. The zoo has a full program of daily events, feeds and talks where visitors can get an insight into the zookeepers' working day.

Gaelic sports are celebrated here; interactive games test the skills of wannabe players

TOP 25

GAA Museum

Located in Croke Park, which is Ireland's most famous sporting venue, this is a place for every sports fan. The ground is the headquarters of the Gaelic Athletic Association (GAA), the country's largest sporting and cultural organization, with a long history.

Exhibits and tours The museum is dedicated to the history and culture of Ireland's national games, especially hurling, Gaelic football and shinty (a team game using a stick and ball, similar to hurling). The exhibition galleries, spread over two floors, include a Hall of Fame dedicated to Ireland's sporting heroes over the ages, plus a vast display of trophies. Dozens of audiovisual, interactive displays look back at the history of these sports from ancient times until today, highlighting their cultural impact on the country and the national identity. There is also an interactive Games Zone to test out your hurling and Gaelic football skills and reflexes. The Croke Park stadium tour, which must be booked separately, includes behind-the-scenes visits to the team dressing rooms, the media center and the players' tunnel—a real spine-tingling experience.

Skyline tour The newest addition to this historic venue is the Etihad Skyline tour, which lies 17 levels high on the roof of the stadium. From here, visitors can walk over the top and take in panoramic views of the city. The tour has a guide, but there are also audio guides available.

THE BASICS

crokepark.ie/gaa-museum

✚ J3

✉ St. Joseph's Avenue

☎ 819 2323

🕐 Jun–Aug Mon–Sat 9.30–6, Sun 10.30–5; Sep–May Mon–Sat 9.30–5, Sun 10.30–5; adjusted schedule on match days

🚌 3, 11, 16, 41 from city center

✋ Expensive

HIGHLIGHTS

● Stadium tour
● Hall of Fame
● Etihad Skyline
● Games Zone

FARTHER AFIELD TOP 25

93

Glasnevin Cemetery and Museum

TOP 25

The museum's sleek glass exterior contrasts sharply with the cemetery's traditional stone Celtic crosses

THE BASICS

glasnevintrust.ie

➕ E1/E2/F1

✉ Finglas Road, Glasnevin

☎ 882 6500

🕐 Mon–Sat 8.30–4.30, Sun 9–4.30

🚉 Drumcondra

🚌 140, 40 from O'Connell Street

♿ Good, except to crypt

🎫 Free; fee for tours

🕑 Tours daily 11.30am and 2.30pm. Special tours daily Mar–Sep at 1pm; Sat–Sun Oct–Feb at 1pm

🍴 Tower Café

The Museum

glasnevinmuseum.ie

☎ 882 6550

🕐 Daily 10–5

💷 Moderate

HIGHLIGHTS

- Guided tours
- Michael Collins' plot
- Daniel O'Connoll's crypt
- Permanent exhibition "City of the Dead"

This enormous cemetery is a veritable Who's Who of modern Ireland's formative years: Charles Stewart Parnell, Michael Collins and Eamon de Valera are buried here, to name but a few.

Cemetery This is also the resting place of poet Gerard Manley Hopkins and writer Brendan Behan, as well as politician and engineer of Catholic Emancipation in Ireland, Daniel O'Connell (1775–1847), who founded the cemetery. Others buried here include thousands of suffragettes, artists and trailblazing women, not to mention the 1.5 million paupers who lie here in unmarked graves. The daily guided tours, led by local experts, show off some of the historic highlights of this Victorian burial ground, pointing out the most attractive headstones and carved Celtic crosses. Book ahead for tours, especially the one at 2.30pm when the famous speech delivered by Patrick Pearse in 1915 is re-enacted by a costumed actor in full uniform.

The museum The new museum, located just inside the cemetery's main entrance, has permanent exhibitions including "City of the Dead" depicting the cemetery's history. There's also a display on how grave robbers would steal corpses—the sturdy watchtowers were later built to prevent such thefts. All the burial and cremation records, from the first burial in 1828 until today, are digitalized and visitors can access them in the genealogy section.

Gallery fountain (left); Snowman by Gary Hume (right)

Irish Museum of Modern Art

The Royal Hospital at Kilmainham, once a haven for retired soldiers, is now an ultramodern cultural hub where regularly changing exhibitions showcase the latest trends in contemporary art.

Shelter The most important surviving 17th-century building in Ireland, the Royal Hospital at Kilmainham was founded as the Irish equivalent of the Invalides in Paris and the Chelsea pensioners' hospital in London. The architect, surveyor-general Sir William Robinson, laid the structure around an open quadrangle, and created a covered arcade around three sides of the ground floor where residents could stroll outdoors even in poor weather.

Transformation A hospital until 1927, the building was restored in 1984 and eventually opened as the Irish Museum of Modern Art in 1991. IMMA is Ireland's leading national institution for the collection and preservation of modern and contemporary works of art. The Permanent Collection of 1,650 works reflects trends in Irish and international art, including installations, video art, sculpture and paintings. The Madden Arnholz Collection comprises old master prints by innovative European print-makers such as Dürer, Rembrandt, Goya and Hogarth, together with books containing prints by Thomas Bewick and his family and one of Bewick's printing blocks. The museum stages changing exhibitions of modern art from Europe and beyond, and is renowned for its education.

THE BASICS

imma.ie

➕ C7

✉ Royal Hospital, Military Road, Kilmainham

☎ 612 9900

🕐 Tue–Sat 10–5.30 (Wed 10.30–5.30), Sun and public hols 12–5.30

🍴 Café

🚉 Heuston

🚌 26, 51, 51B, 78A, 79, 90, 123; Luas Heuston

♿ Good

🎟 Free

❓ Free guided tours every afternoon. Well-stocked bookshop

HIGHLIGHTS

● Covered arcade
● Courtyard with sculptures
● Permanent collections
● Visiting exhibitions

FARTHER AFIELD   TOP 25

Kilmainham Gaol

TOP 25

The pedestrian avenue leading to Kilmainham (left); the main gaol compound is now a museum (right)

HIGHLIGHTS

● East wing
● 1916 corridor with cells
● Museum display

TIP

● Ask the guide to shut you into one of the cells and find out what prison life was like.

Leading figures in every rebellion against British rule since 1798 are associated with Kilmainham Gaol and, for many Irish people, their imprisonment or death represents freedom through sacrifice.

Prisoners With its stark and severe interiors, Kilmainham has a fascination that is more inspirational than morbid. Opened in 1796, and altered frequently since, the gaol is made up of tall interlinked blocks in the middle, flanked by exercise and work yards. During the course of its long history it held both civil and political prisoners, the earliest of whom were participants in the 1798 rebellion. The flow continued throughout the following century and included the "Young Ireland" rebels of 1848 (Europe's "Year of Revolution"), the Fenian suspects of 1867 and notable parliamentarians in the 1880s.

Conditions Overcrowding created appalling conditions when the Great Famine of 1845–49 drove many to petty crime. Closed in 1910, the gaol was reopened during the 1916 rebellion in Dublin to receive insurgents whose execution in the prison in the May and June of that year turned the tide of public opinion in many parts of Ireland in favor of the armed struggle. During the Civil War of the early 1920s, the gaol again housed anti-government rebels including many women, and four Republican leaders were executed. The doors were finally closed in 1924. The gaol is now cared for by the State and has an excellent museum display.

CASINO MARINO

casinomarino.ie

The Mediterranean-inspired Casino is a compact and ingenious 18th-century architectural creation. Its patron was James Caulfield, fourth Viscount Charlemont (1728–99), whose travels inspired the elegant design. Its floor plan is a Greek cross encircled by pillars on a raised podium, with lions at each corner creating a diagonal axis. The four state rooms boast curving wooden doors, stucco friezes and marquetry floors made from rare woods.

➕ M1 ✉ Cherrymount Crescent, off the Malahide Road, Marino ☎ 833 1618 🕒 Mar–Oct daily 10–5; last admission 45 mins before closing 🚆 Clontarf Road 🚌 14, 20A, 20B, 27A ♿ Few 🎟 Inexpensive ❓ Visit by guided tour only

IRISH JEWISH MUSEUM

jewishmuseum.ie

In a former synagogue, the museum is dedicated to the history of the Jewish community in Ireland from the mid-19th century to the present day. The original kitchen re-creates a typical Sabbath meal of the early 20th century.

➕ G9 ✉ 3 Walworth Road, off Victoria Street ☎ 490 1857 🕒 Nov–Apr Sun only 10.30–2.30; May–Oct Sun, Tue, Thu 11–3 🚌 16, 16A, 19, 19A, 122 ♿ Few 🎟 Free

JAMES JOYCE TOWER AND MUSEUM

joycetower.ie

Featured at the beginning of Joyce's *Ulysses*, this tower is one of many 19th-century Martello towers on Ireland's east coast and is prominent in the annual Bloomsday celebrations (▷ 114). The museum displays Joycean memorabilia.

➕ See map ▷ 91 ✉ Sandycove Point, Glenageary ☎ 280 9265 🕒 Daily 10–6 in summer; 10–4 in winter 🚆 Dun Laoghaire ♿ Few 🎟 Free

NATIONAL BOTANIC GARDENS

botanicgardens.ie

Founded in 1795, these huge gardens contain Ireland's most extensive and varied collection of plants. The curvilinear glasshouses, built by Richard Turner, a Dubliner who created a similar one for Kew Gardens in London, are among the finest surviving examples of 19th-century glass-and-iron construction. Many of the plants housed within originate from southeast Asia. See herbaceous borders, alpines, roses, the rock garden, pond and arboretum.

➕ F1 ✉ Glasnevin Hill Road ☎ 804 0300 🕒 Mar–Oct Mon–Fri 9–5, Sat–Sun and public hols 10–6; Nov–Feb Mon–Fri 9–4.30, Sat–Sun and public hols 10–4.30 🚆 Drumcondra 🚌 4, 9 ♿ Good except for some glasshouses 🎟 Free; fee for parking

Casino Marino

NATIONAL TRANSPORT MUSEUM

nationaltransportmuseum.org

Located at the Heritage Depot, this museum houses a charming selection of historic vehicles from Ireland, including century-old trams and an 1883 Merryweather fire appliance. There is also a fleet of military vehicles, including World War II classics.

➕ See map ▷ 91 ✉ Heritage Depot, Howth Demesne ☎ 832 0427 ⏰ Sat–Sun and public hols 2–5 🚉 Howth 💷 Inexpensive

PEARSE MUSEUM

pearsemuseum.ie

This former school was run by Patrick Pearse, the Dublin-born poet and revolutionary executed in 1916 at Kilmainham Gaol (▷ 96). It has a nature study room displaying Irish fauna and flora. Concerts are held here in summer. It's set in beautiful grounds in St. Enda's Park.

➕ See map ▷ 90 ✉ St. Enda's Park, Grange Road, Rathfarnham ☎ 493 4208

⏰ Mar–Oct Mon–Sat 9.30–5.30; Nov–Jan 9.30–4, Feb 9.30–5, Sun and public hols from 10 🚌 16 🍴 Tea rooms ♿ Few 💷 Free

PHOENIX PARK

phoenixpark.ie

A vast green expanse in the heart of the city, this is one of the largest urban parks in Europe, covering some 707ha (1,747 acres) and encircled by a 13km (8-mile) wall. Within its confines are Dublin Zoo (▷ 92), the American Ambassador's home and the Irish President's residence. Bicycles are available to rent.

➕ A5 ☎ 820 5800 ⏰ Gates open daily 24-hours 🚌 37, 38, 39; Luas Heuston (Parkgate Street entrance) 💷 Free

WAR MEMORIAL GARDENS

heritageireland.ie

These gardens are dedicated to the 49,400 Irish soldiers who died in WWI, with thousands of names etched in the granite book rooms.

➕ A7 ✉ Islandbridge ☎ 475 7816 ⏰ Mon–Fri 8–dusk, Sat–Sun 10–dusk 🚌 51, 68, 69 💷 Free

Golden harp at the War Memorial Gardens (above); Dublin Zoo (right)

FARTHER AFIELD MORE TO SEE

DUBLIN AREA RAPID TRANSIT

Dublin from the DART

VIEWS FROM THE DART

- Dalkey Island off Killiney
- Sailboats off Dun Laoghaire
- Blackrock's public park and private gardens
- Wetlands bird sanctuary at Booterstown
- Custom House between Tara Street and Connolly Station
- Urban jungle of Kilbarrack, backdrop for novels *The Commitments*, *The Snapper* and *The Van*, Roddy Doyle's prize-winning trilogy

BRAY

This attractive seaside town, toward the southern end of the DART line, has long been a popular holiday resort enjoyed for its sandy beach and mile-long promenade. The Jazz Festival in May and summer events bring in the crowds. There are well-marked walks and great views around nearby Bray Head.

DUN LAOGHAIRE

Invigorating walks along the piers at Dun Laoghaire, a Victorian seaside resort once known as Kingstown, are something of a Dublin institution. The scenery is stunning, and you can see the ferries plying across the Irish Sea. The East Pier has a lighthouse at the end and the West Pier attracts fishing enthusiasts. There are good seafood restaurants here, plus the National Maritime Museum of Ireland.

HOWTH

This promontory to the north of Dublin is a traditional fishing village and fashionable suburb, and is especially lovely on a sunny day. A popular sailing hub, the marina is always packed with yachts from Ireland and abroad. Howth DART station is near the harbor and close to all the waterside activity, bars and restaurants.

Fishing boats in the harbor at Howth

Bray Head promenade (above right);
Kilruddery House, Bray (right)

KILLINEY

Celebrities such as Bono, Damon Hill, Neil Jordan and Van Morrison have lived in the resort known affectionately as Dublin's Riviera. Take a walk along the Vico Road for what is arguably the most breathtaking view in Dublin. Look out to Dalkey Island, a craggy piece of land captured by the Vikings and later the site of Christian communities. Fishermen in nearby Coliemore Harbour run boat trips in summer to view the resident goats, the ruined oratory and the Martello tower.

SANDYCOVE

Just south of Dun Laoghaire and accessible by the DART is the popular village of Sandycove, famous for its seaside promenade, which runs all the way to Dun Laoghaire. It is named after a small sandy cove near the rocky point on which a Martello tower was built during the Napoleonic Wars. James Joyce chose the Martello tower along the waterfront as the setting for the first chapter of *Ulysses,* and the museum inside (▷ 97) displays much Joycean memorabilia. It features each June in the "Bloomsday" festival, which celebrates the hero of *Ulysses*. A bracing swim in the sea here may introduce you to other die-hards who take the plunge all year around.

DALKEY

Travel only a few stops south on the DART and you'll find yourself in the attractive former fishing village of Dalkey, well known for its literary associations. George Bernard Shaw lived in the village and James Joyce set chapter two of *Ulysses* here. The Heritage Centre is accessed through Goat Castle in Castle Street and from the battlements you get a splendid view of the sea and mountains. Good pubs and restaurants enhance your visit.

View from Dalkey Hill across Killiney Bay toward the distant Wicklow hills

Excursions

THE BASICS

heritageireland.ie
Distance: 50km (31 miles)
Journey Time: 1 hour 30 mins
✉ Brú Na Bóinne Visitor Centre, Donore, Co Meath
☎ 041 988 0300
🕐 Jun–Sep daily 9–7; Oct, Feb-Apr 9.30–5.30; May 9–6.30; Nov–Jan 9-5
🚌 Bus Éireann 100 to Drogheda, then 163 to Donore village (10-min walk). Also bus tours

BRÚ NA BÓINNE

A designated UNESCO World Heritage Site, Brú Na Bóinne is one of the most important prehistoric monuments in Europe. "The Palace of the Boyne" is the name given to a large group of neolithic remains in the central Boyne Valley, 11km (7 miles) west of Drogheda and 50km (31 miles northwest) of Dublin. The huge, white-fronted Newgrange is the best known, a 5,200-year-old passage tomb, leading to a chamber with three alcoves. The nearby mound of Knowth (northwest) was of similar importance, historically. These great tombs can only be visited with a guided tour and in small groups leaving from the visitor center, where visitor numbers are limited (booking ahead is advisable).

THE BASICS

glendalough.ie
Distance: 48km (30 miles)
Journey Time: 1 hour 15 mins
☎ 404 45325
🕐 Visitor center mid-Mar to mid-Oct daily 9.30–6; mid-Oct to mid-Mar 9.30–5; last admission 45 mins before closing
🚌 St. Kevin's bus from Bray and Dublin. Can be reached on coach tours from Dublin. The most direct route if driving is the N11 (M11) south

GLENDALOUGH

Glendalough ("valley of two lakes") was one of Ireland's most venerated monastic sites. Its spectacular setting makes it one of eastern Ireland's premier attractions, lying 48km (31 miles) south of Dublin. Situated at the end of a long valley stretching deep into the Wicklow Mountains, Glendalough grew up around the tomb of its founder, St. Kevin. He was abbot until his death in AD618 and this early Christian monastery became famous throughout Europe as a seat of learning. The core of the old monastery consists of a roofless cathedral (c900), a well-preserved Round Tower (30m/98ft high) and St. Kevin's Church, roofed with stone and with a 12th-century round tower belfry. Overlooking the Upper Lake is another enchanting church called Reefert. There are good walks in the surrounding woods and it can get very busy in high summer. The visitor center also acts as an information outlet for the Wicklow Mountains National Park.

MALAHIDE CASTLE

In the pretty seaside town of Malahide, this stunning castle, set on 250 acres of parkland, stayed mainly in the hands of the Talbot family from 1185 until 1973. The core of the castle is a medieval tower, and in the adjoining banqueting hall the walls are hung with magnificent Irish portraits. Most of the period furnishings are from the Georgian era. Enjoy a tour of the castle rooms, including the Oak Room, and Great Hall. Also explore the walled gardens at your own pace, and the beautiful Talbot Botanic Gardens that were mainly created by Lord Milo Talbot in the mid-20th century. There is also an Avoca gift shop and café (▷ panel, 106), plus the visitor center in the courtyard.

THE BASICS

malahidecastleandgardens.ie

Distance: 13km (8 miles)
Journey Time: 45 mins
☎ 846 2184
🕐 Daily 9.30–4.30 (last tour); Nov–Mar 9.30–3.30. Guided tours every hour
🚌 42
🚆 From Connolly Station to Malahide, then a 10-min walk

POWERSCOURT

Beautifully set in the heart of the wild Wicklow Mountains, yet only an hour away from Dublin, this house is renowned for its magnificent Italianate gardens. Careful restoration has converted the 18th-century Palladian mansion into an excellent Avoca store (▷ panel, 106) with a terrace café. It is in a dramatic setting, with the cone-shape Sugar Loaf mountain in the distance. To the south, the house looks out over magnificent stepped terraces, with ornamental sculpture and a statue throwing a jet of water high in the air. Gardens stretch to either side; the one to the east is Japanese, the other walled, with wrought-iron gates. There is also a huge pet cemetery. (The story goes that when the terraces' designer, Daniel Robertson, went to inspect the work every morning, he was pushed around in a wheelbarrow, swigging sherry.) The waterfall is a short drive (5km/ 3 miles) away and is the highest waterfall in Ireland and there is an additional entrance fee to pay.

THE BASICS

powerscourt.ie

Distance: 19km (12 miles)
Journey Time: 1 hour
☎ 204 6000
🕐 Daily 9.30–5.30 (gardens close at dusk in winter)
🚌 44 to Enniskerry, then walk
🚆 DART to Bray, then 185 feeder bus to Enniskerry
❓ Waterfall inadvisable to reach on foot as the footpath is incomplete

Shopping

BLACKROCK MARKET

blackrockmarket.com

Bargain hunters flock to Blackrock, 8km (5 miles) south of Dublin, for the market held every Saturday 11–5.30 and Sunday 12–5.30 (also holiday Mondays 11–5.30). Stalls sell clothes, bric-à-brac, fine art, crafts and antiques. There are usually around 50 traders, plus refreshment stands.

➕ Off map ✉ Blackrock ☎ 283 3522
🚆 Blackrock 🚌 G7, 7A, 8, 17

DUNDRUM TOWN CENTRE

dundrum.ie

A 22-minute ride away on the Luas, this is one of the largest and most modern shopping venues in Ireland. There are more than 120 stores, with big names such as Harvey Nichols and House of Fraser, restaurants, cafés and bars. There is also a 12-screen cinema and a multi-functional arts venue, the Mill Theatre.

➕ Off map ✉ Sandyford Road, Dundrum
☎ 299 1700 🚌 17, 14A; Luas Sandyford

LIFFEY VALLEY SHOPPING CENTRE

liffeyvalley.ie

A 20-minute drive southwest of Dublin, with more than 90 retail outlets, including Tommy Hilfiger and Diesel. The food court has many restaurants and cafés, and there is also a multiscreen cinema.

➕ Off map ✉ Fonthill Road, Clontalkin
🚌 25, 66, 78A

NAUGHTON BOOKSELLERS

naughtonsbooks.com

Browse this family-run bookstore crammed with thousands of antiquarian and rare books. There's also Irish-interest material, plus travel, religion and art.

➕ Off map ✉ 8 Marine Terrace, Dun Laoghaire ☎ 280 4392 🚆 Dun Laoghaire, Sandycove, Glasthule

Entertainment and Nightlife

THE ABBEY TAVERN

abbeytavern.ie

A famous Howth venue, The Abbey has a centuries-old history, complete with flagged floors and open fires. There is traditional music and dancing, plus good food. Choose from a selection of Irish whiskeys and craft beers.

➕ Off map ✉ 28 Abbey Street, Howth
☎ 839 0307 🚆 Howth

CIVIC THEATRE

civictheatre.ie

A community arts venue in the southwest suburbs providing contemporary drama, dance, opera and classical music. You can also view the small art collection or have a drink in the theatre's cosy bistro.

➕ Off map ✉ Blessington Road, off Belguard Square East, Tallaght ☎ 462 7477 🚌 49, 50, 54A, 65, 77; Luas Tallaght

GAELIC GAMES

gaa.ie; crokepark.ie

The traditional sports of Gaelic football and hurling are fast, physical games, and the All-Ireland finals are played before sell-out crowds at Croke Park (▷ 93) in early and late September.

These matches are immensely popular with locals and visitors alike and tickets sell out very quickly.

🏬 J3 ✉ Croke Park Stadium, St. Joseph's Avenue ☎ 819 2300 🚌 11, 16, 51A

THE HELIX
thehelix.ie

This modern arts complex at the City University has three auditoria—the 1,260-capacity Mahony Hall, the 450-seat Theatre and the 150-seat Space. It serves up a mixed program of classical concerts, drama and ballet, plus rock and pop music.

🏬 Off map ✉ Dublin City University, Collins Avenue, Glasnevin ☎ 700 7000 🚌 4, 11, 13, 16, 44

HORSE RACING
leopardstown.com

Leopardstown Race Course is one of Ireland's busiest. It hosts the Irish Gold Cup and a traditional post-Christmas festival, among other events.

🏬 Off map ✉ Leopardstown ☎ 289 0500 🚋 Luas Sandyford

JOHN KAVANAGH

Adjacent to Glasnevin Cemetery, this cosy, family pub is known by locals as the "Gravediggers." Apparently it was where workers would head for a pint after their duties. Little has changed inside since it opened in 1833. It serves good, home-cooked food.

🏬 G1 ✉ 1 Prospect Square ☎ 830 7978 🚌 13, 19, 40

JOHNNIE FOX'S
jfp.ie

Popular with visitors from near and far and for its turf fires, live traditional music, *céilí* dancing and tasty seafood. If you want to eat, reserve ahead.

🏬 Off map ✉ Glencullen ☎ 295 5647 🚌 Special express bus—reservations advisable (☎ 822 1122, expressbus.ie)

RUGBY
avivastadium.ie; irishrugby.ie

Ireland's fans are always enthusiastic when it comes to their national team. Details of fixtures for local clubs, like Bective Rangers and Wesley, are published in the local press. The Aviva Stadium, built on the site of the old Lansdowne Road Stadium, opened in 2010 and is the home of Ireland's national rugby team. The huge Six Nations tournament sees at least one match here in Feb–Mar. Or you could watch a game in one of the many pubs.

🏬 M9 ✉ Aviva Lansdowne Road Stadium, Ballsbridge ☎ 647 3800 🚉 Lansdowne Road 🚌 5, 7, 7A, 45

SOCCER
fai.ie; tallaghtstadium.ie

Since the FIFA World Cup in 1990, the Irish have become soccer fanatics, and Dublin pauses when the national team plays. The domestic season runs from March to November. You can buy tickets for matches involving Ireland's most successful team, Shamrock Rovers' (Tallaght Stadium) at the gate.

🏬 Off map ✉ Tallaght Stadium, Whitestown Way ☎ 460 5948 🚌 49, 65; Luas Tallaght

GOLF

The growth in the number of championship golf courses in Dublin is staggering. Many clubs welcome non-members, and fees are reasonable. The most famous are Portmarnock (▷ 111) and Royal Dublin; also try Castle, Grange, Malahide, Hermitage and Island, or try one of the city's pitch-and-putt courses.

Where to Eat

AQUA (€€–€€€)

aqua.ie

Aqua wins top prize for its spectacular
location, at the end of the pier, overlooking the sea. It's known for its excellent
seafood, with fresh fish caught locally,
plus some Irish game dishes. The food
is matched with very good service.
➕ Off map ✉ 1 West Pier, Howth
☎ 832 0690 🕐 Lunch and dinner Tue–Sun
🚆 Howth

AVOCA SALT CAFÉ (€)

avoca.com

This bright and airy café is attached to
the fabulous Food Market. The menu
is globally influenced using local produce, from Persian lamb casserole to
Wicklow venison.
➕ Off map ✉ 11A The Crescent, Monkstown
☎ 202 0230 🕐 Breakfast, lunch and dinner
daily 🚆 Monkstown

CAVISTONS (€€)

cavistons.com

Cavistons is a highly regarded gourmet
seafood restaurant. The sophisticated
menu changes daily.
➕ Off map ✉ 59 Glasthule Road, Sandycove
☎ 280 9245 🕐 Lunch Tue–Sat, dinner Fri, Sat
(6–8pm) 🚆 Sandycove and Glasthule 🚌 59

HARTLEY'S (€€–€€€)

hartleys.ie

Enjoy a sophisticated setting for fish,
prime steak and seafood here, where
you can dine overlooking the harbor.

➕ Off map ✉ 1 Harbour Road, Dun
Laoghaire ☎ 280 6767 🕐 Lunch and dinner
Tue–Sun 🚆 Dun Laoghaire 🚌 7

HERON & GREY (€€€)

heronandgrey.com

Awarded its first Michelin star in 2016,
it's difficult to get a reservation at this
tiny restaurant but those that do are
rewarded with a three-hour dining
extravaganza. Using local seasonal ingredients, it serves modern international
cuisine with five-course tasting menus.
➕ Off map ✉ 19a Main Street, Blackrock
☎ 212 3676 🕐 Dinner Thu–Sat 🚆 Blackrock

KING SITRIC (€€€)

kingsitric.ie

The fish are landed a few yards from
Dublin's most regal seafood restaurant,
named after Dublin's 11th-century
Norse king. Going strong for more than
40 years, it's popular with Dublin high
society with a wonderful menu and
wine cellar. The more casual East Café
Bar is on the same site.
➕ Off map ✉ East Pier, Howth ☎ 832
5235 🕐 Restaurant: dinner Wed–Sat, lunch
Sun. Cafe: lunch and dinner daily 🚆 Howth
🚌 31, 31B

AVOCA CAFÉS

The Avoca Handweavers were founded in
1723, and in recent years their award-
winning cafés have been talked about as
much as their famous shops. You can find
branches in the village of Avoca, the home
of the original mill, at Kilmacanoge near
Bray, at Powerscourt House (▷ 103)
and in the middle of Dublin in Suffolk
Street. Homemade is the key word and
the delicious desserts are especially
noteworthy, along with great scones,
cookies and cakes.

FARTHER AFIELD WHERE TO EAT

From boutique hotels to elegant Georgian town houses, there are some great choices when deciding where to stay in Dublin. North of the river, staying in a bed-and-breakfast is a less-expensive option.

Introduction

As you'd expect from a lively, modern and cosmopolitan capital, Dublin offers every type and style of place to stay. There is a huge choice, from budget hotels and self-catering to good-value Georgian town houses converted into charming hotels or guesthouses, fashionable boutique hotels and luxury 5-star establishments. Don't be afraid to choose a place in the suburbs; room rates are lower and the city's public transportation system is efficient.

Accommodations Options

Exclusive hotels in the heart of the city, in particular around St. Stephen's Green and Merrion Square, offer high standards and prices to match. For decent quality and value, try the town house hotels or stay in the quieter suburbs such as leafy Ballsbridge (Dublin 4), known as the embassy area. A short bus ride or 15-minute walk into town, it is also convenient for the Aviva Stadium at Lansdowne Road, 3Arena, Financial Centre and Docklands.

Reservation Advice

Many visitors make their accommodations booking online, and it is useful to compare several websites, including that of the hotel itself. During special events like rugby and soccer internationals and St. Patrick's Day, the city gets very busy, and hotel rates rise accordingly—book as far ahead as possible. Prices sometimes include a full Irish breakfast, but many places now offer room-only rates. If you have not booked in advance, Dublin Tourism in Suffolk Street offers an on-the-spot booking service, for Dublin and the whole of Ireland.

SELF-CATERING

Most self-catering options are in the suburbs or at the coast, but there are some in the city. Check out visitdublin.com, which is a good place to start your search for whatever style of accommodations you are seeking.

Budget Hotels

ARIEL HOUSE

ariel-house.net

Occupying two gracious Victorian town houses in a peaceful suburb, this hotel has good standard guest rooms. It's known for its tasty breakfasts—with vegetarian options—and friendly service.

L9 ⊠ 50–54 Lansdowne Road, Ballsbridge ☎ 668 5512 🚊 Lansdowne Road 🚌 7, 45

CLAYTON HOTEL BALLSBRIDGE

claytonhotelballsbridge.com

The building of this good-value hotel in Ballsbridge, formerly Bewley's Hotel, is a former 19th-century Masonic school. Rooms are bright and spacious, with gardens, and there are family rooms available. It is close to the RDS, a 20-minute walk to the city center, and the Aircoach stop is right outside.

Off map ⊠ Merrion Road ☎ 668 1111 🚌 4, 7

JURY'S INN PARNELL SQUARE

jurysinns.com

Part of the reputable Jury's group, this one has a central location north of the Liffey, close to O'Connell Street. It presents 253 good-value, spacious rooms, some of which can sleep two adults and two children.

G5 ⊠ Moore Street Plaza, Parnell Street ☎ 878 4900 🚌 Cross-city buses

MALDRON HOTEL SMITHFIELD

maldronhotelsmithfield.com

This great-value hotel in the heart of Smithfield is just a few steps from the famous music pub The Cobblestone (▷ 60), and close to the Luas stop.

The rooms here are bright and cheerful, some with a balcony, and have views of the city center.

F6 ⊠ Smithfield ☎ 485 0900 🚊 Luas Smithfield

MARIAN GUEST HOUSE

marianguesthouse.ie

In a Georgian town house close to central Dublin, this family-run place offers good value and free parking.

H4 ⊠ 21 Gardiner Street Upper ☎ 874 4129 🚊 Connolly 🚌 41A

OLIVER ST. JOHN GOGARTY

gogartys.ie

The apartments here sleep up to four people, with a shared bathroom. This is a very central location in Temple Bar but be prepared for a lively stay, with the bar and restaurant here always packed and plenty of traditional music played in the upstairs bar.

H7 ⊠ 18–21 Anglesea Street ☎ 671 1822 🚊 Connolly 🚌 Cross-city buses

O'SHEAS

osheashotel.com

In a landmark Georgian building, especially handy for Connolly station, this family-run hotel has a popular Irish music bar downstairs.

H5 ⊠ 19 Talbot Street ☎ 836 5670 🚊 Connolly 🚌 Cross-city buses

TRINITY COLLEGE

tcd.ie

If you are planning a stay in the summer (late May to mid-Sep), it is possible to rent student rooms in Trinity College at reasonable rates. Most are three to four bedrooms, sharing a small kitchen, living room and bathroom.

H7 ⊠ College Green ☎ 896 4477 🚊 Pearse, Tara Street 🚌 Cross-city buses

Mid-Range Hotels

ABERDEEN LODGE
aberdeen-lodge.com
A short DART ride from central Dublin, this fine Edwardian house with 16 en suite rooms ensures a comfortable stay in a quiet suburb. Some of the rooms have four-poster beds.

Off map 🖂 53 Park Avenue, Sandymount 🕾 283 8155 🚇 Sydney Parade

BROOKS HOTEL
brookshotel.ie
This centrally located boutique hotel boasts a 26-seat private cinema, plus guest rooms furnished with Irish wooden furniture, with touches such as dressmakers' mannequins. Its Jasmine Bar hosts special whiskey tasting events.

G7 🖂 Drury Street 🕾 670 4000 🚌 Cross-city buses; Luas St. Stephen's Green

BUSWELLS
buswells.ie
Comprising five grandiose Georgian town houses, Buswells is one of Dublin's oldest hotels. Buswell's bar is a popular meeting place for MPs from the Dáil opposite.

H7 🖂 23–25 Molesworth Street 🕾 614 6500 🚇 Pearse 🚌 Cross-city buses

CASSIDY'S HOTEL
cassidyshotel.com
Family-run, this 119-room hotel in a Georgian terrace sits at the top end of O'Connell Street. Grooms Bar and Bistro are an added bonus. The executive wing has a fitness suite.

H5 🖂 6–8 Cavendish Row, O'Connell Street Upper 🕾 878 0555 🚌 Cross-city buses

DEER PARK HOTEL GOLF & SPA
deerpark-hotel.ie
Only 14km (8.5 miles) from central Dublin, this hotel is located on a quiet hillside in the grounds of Howth Castle and overlooking the sea. Large golf complex and spa.

Off map 🖂 Howth 🕾 832 2624 🚇 Howth

GRAFTON CAPITAL
graftoncapitalhotel.com
The 75 spacious rooms at this hotel are at the heart of Dublin's shopping and cultural area. In a traditional Georgian town house, this is a good-value hotel.

G7 🖂 Stephen's Street Lower 🕾 648 1100 🚇 Pearse 🚌 Cross-city buses

GRAND CANAL HOTEL
grandcanalhotel.ie
Part of the new canal complex, this purpose-built hotel has 142 rooms and is conveniently situated for the 3Arena and Aviva Stadium.

L8 🖂 Upper Grand Canal Street 🕾 646 1000 🚇 Grand Canal Dock 🚌 5, 7, 7A, 8, 18, 27X, 45

HARRINGTON HALL
harringtonhall.com
This is a beautiful Georgian guesthouse, with genteel public areas and generously proportioned guest rooms.

G9 🖂 70 Harcourt Street 🕾 475 3497 🚌 Cross-city buses

JURY'S INN CHRISTCHURCH
jurysinns.com
Opposite Christ Church Cathedral, the 182 modern guest rooms here are of decent size. There are some family rooms and spacious executive rooms.

K7 🖂 Christchurch Place 🕾 454 0000 🚌 Cross-city buses

MESPIL HOTEL

mespilhotel.com

With a quiet location on the Grand Canal, and a short walk to the city center, this efficient and modern hotel has a great selection of spacious family rooms, some sleeping up to five guests.

➕ J9 ✉ 50–60 Mespil Road ☎ 488 4600 🚇 Grand Canal Dock 🚌 10

MOLESWORTH COURT SUITES

molesworthcourt.ie

These contemporary suites and penthouses are located on a quiet street close to Grafton Street. The largest ones sleep six, with a well-equipped kitchen and living room.

➕ H8 ✉ Schoolhouse Lane, off Molesworth Street ☎ 676 4799 🚇 Pearse 🚌 Cross-city buses

THE MORGAN

themorgan.com

Spacious bathrooms and excellent in-room facilities are the hallmarks in this luxurious boutique hotel. The bar here is very popular. Guests can enjoy free use of the nearby gym and pool.

➕ H6 ✉ 10 Fleet Street, Temple Bar ☎ 643 7000 🚇 Tara Street 🚌 Cross-city buses

THE PARLIAMENT HOTEL

parliamenthotel.ie

Close to the historic Fishamble Street, and around the corner from lively nightlife in Temple Bar, this smart hotel has spacious guest rooms. There is live traditional music each night in the bar.

➕ G7 ✉ 16–18 Lord Edward Street ☎ 670 8777 🚌 Cross-city buses

THE SCHOOLHOUSE HOTEL

schoolhousehotel.com

The product of an excellent conversion from a school, dating back to 1859, the

GOLF HOTELS

Ireland's reputation as a world class golfing destination is undisputed; and there are some excellent hotels with great courses just outside the city. Try the Portmarnock Hotel and Golf Links, renowned for comfort, good food and world-class golf. The hotel's 18-hole course was designed by Bernard Langer. Conveniently close to the airport.

➕ Off map ✉ Strand Road, Portmarnock ☎ 846 0611; portmarnock.com

For another golf hotel option, see the opposite page for the Deer Park Hotel.

31 boutique guest rooms here are simple and tastefully designed. Each is dedicated to prominent names in Irish history. The hotel also has an excellent restaurant and bar.

➕ K8 ✉ 2–8 Northumberland Road ☎ 667 5014 🚇 Grand Canal Dock 🚌 Cross-city buses

STAUNTONS ON THE GREEN

stauntonsonthegreen.ie

Many famous names have lived in this Georgian town house, including prominent poets, politicians and priests. It is one of Dublin's favorites, with 30 spacious guest rooms and a garden, close to the city's museums and shops.

➕ H8 ✉ 83 St. Stephen's Green ☎ 478 2300 🚇 Pearse 🚌 Cross-city buses

WYNN'S HOTEL

wynnshotel.ie

Housed in a listed building, this large hotel is near many of north Dublin's theaters and has enjoyed a long literary history. The guest rooms are elegant and simple. Facilities also include a fitness room.

➕ H6 ✉ 35–39 Lower Abbey Street ☎ 874 5131 🚌 Cross-city buses; Luas Abbey Street

Luxury Hotels

CLARENCE

theclarence.ie

The chic, modern interior with stunning floral arrangements creates a stylish environment. The 50 rooms are small, apart from the fine duplex penthouse.

➕ G7 ✉ 6–8 Wellington Quay ☎ 407 0800 🚇 Tara Street 🚌 Cross-city buses

THE DAWSON HOTEL & SPA

thedawson.ie

There are 28 individually designed rooms and suites in this luxury boutique hotel. The spa offers holistic therapies.

➕ H8 ✉ 35 Dawson Street ☎ 677 4444 🚌 Cross-city buses

DYLAN

dylan.ie

Boutique hotel with 44 glamorous rooms and suites. First-rate facilities and plenty of style. Smart restaurant, buzzy bar.

➕ K9 ✉ Eastmoreland Place ☎ 660 3000 🚌 10

FITZWILLIAM

fitzwilliamhoteldublin.com

Contemporary style and Irish warmth combine in a central location. Some of the 130 bedrooms overlook an internal rooftop garden.

➕ H8 ✉ St. Stephen's Green ☎ 478 7000 🚇 Pearse 🚌 Cross-city buses

GRESHAM

gresham-hotels.com

The 288 elegant bedrooms partner traditional style with modern comfort. There are several bars and lounges, the Gallery restaurant and use of a gym.

➕ H5 ✉ 23 O'Connell Street Upper ☎ 874 6881 🚇 Connolly 🚌 Cross-city buses

HERBERT PARK

herbertparkhotel.ie

Enjoy quiet comfort in this bright and airy hotel in Dublin's exclusive residential neighborhood. Many of the 153 rooms overlook the peaceful Herbert Park.

➕ Off map ✉ Herbert Park, Ballsbridge ☎ 667 2200 🚇 Lansdowne Road 🚌 7, 45

MERRION

merrionhotel.com

Originally four Georgian houses, the Merrion has 140 luxurious bedrooms. Guests can enjoy the gym, pool, spa and business facilities.

➕ J8 ✉ Merrion Street Upper ☎ 603 0600 🚇 Pearse 🚌 Cross-city buses

THE MORRISON

morrisonhotel.ie

A modern designer heaven, the Morrison offers 138 rooms, suites and studios, plus lobby bars and restaurants. There's also a stunning penthouse.

➕ G6 ✉ Ormond Quay Lower ☎ 887 4200 🚌 Cross-city buses

THE SHELBOURNE

marriott.co.uk

The illustrious Shelbourne Hotel, built in 1824, boasts 265 luxurious rooms. Also there is excellent food in the Saddle Room and Oyster Bar (▷ 88).

➕ H8 ✉ 27 St. Stephen's Green ☎ 663 4500 🚇 Pearse 🚌 Cross-city buses

WESTBURY

doylecollection.com

A stylish hotel with 205 rooms in Dublin's premier shopping street.

➕ H7 ✉ Grafton Street ☎ 679 1122 🚇 Pearse 🚌 Cross-city buses

Baile Átha Cliath km
DUBLIN 26

Gleann Crī km
GLENCREE 8

Dublin is compact and easy to get around on foot. However, buses are numerous and frequent, and the DART is great to use for a trip outside the city. Dublin is a fairly safe city, but keep alert against petty crime.

Planning Ahead

When to Go

Most visitors come between March and October, when the weather is at its best and there is a wider choice of activities. A few attractions are closed in the winter. Dublin is temperate year-round but rain is frequent.

TIME

Ireland is five hours ahead of New York, eight hours ahead of Los Angeles and the same as London.

AVERAGE DAILY MAXIMUM TEMPERATURES

JAN	FEB	MAR	APR	MAY	JUN	JUL	AUG	SEP	OCT	NOV	DEC
46°F	46°F	50°F	55°F	59°F	64°F	68°F	66°F	63°F	57°F	50°F	46°F
8°C	8°C	10°C	13°C	15°C	18°C	20°C	19°C	17°C	14°C	10°C	8°C

Spring (March to May) is mild with mostly clear skies and a mix of sunshine and showers. April and May are the driest months.

Summer (June to August) is bright and warm but notoriously unpredictable. July is particularly showery. Heat waves are rare.

Autumn (September to November) often has very heavy rain and is mostly overcast, although still quite mild. Even October can be summery.

Winter (December to February) is not usually severe and tends to be wet rather than snowy. Temperatures rarely fall below freezing.

WHAT'S ON

January *Tradfest Temple Bar.*
February *Dublin International Film Festival.*
February/March *Six Nations Rugby* at Aviva Stadium.
March *St. Patrick's Day Festival* (several days around 17 Mar).
May *Dublin Dance Festival. Docklands Summer Festival. Dublin Gay Theatre Festival.*
June *Taste of Dublin* (food festival, Iveagh Gardens).
Bloomsday (around 16 Jun): celebration of hero of James Joyce's novel *Ulysses.*
Pride: week-long gay festival.
June–August *Music in parks.*

July–August *Movies on the Square* in Temple Bar every Saturday.
Late August/early September *Liffey Swim. All-Ireland Hurling and Gaelic Football Finals* at Croke Park.
September/October *Dublin Theatre Festival. Dublin Fringe Festival. Irish Champions Weekend—Leopardstown.*
October *Dublin Marathon. Samhain Festival:* parade and fireworks (31 Oct). *Bram Stoker Festival.*
December *National Crafts and Design Fair.*

Christmas carols, concerts: in churches around the city. *New Year's Eve festival,* including ringing bells at midnight at Christ Church Cathedral.

Listings
Daily newspapers cover what's on in Dublin. Look for *The Event Guide,* free from clubs, cafés and restaurants around the city.

Dublin online

visitdublin.com
The local tourist board site unveils every aspect of the city via its efficient search engine. You'll find up-to-date information on accommodations (reserve online), restaurants, shopping, nightlife and attractions, as well as insider guides and downloadable city walking tours.

irishtimes.com
Influential website of the *Irish Times*, one of Dublin's daily newspapers. Read up on the news, weather and what's on.

irish-architecture.com
The Dublin section under Buildings of Ireland is particularly useful (via Leinster).

dublinevents.com
A comprehensive guide about forthcoming events at venues across Dublin, from theater and cinema to live music, comedy, concerts, exhibitions and sports. Plus hotels, restaurants, clubbing *et al*.

dublin-culture.com
Another all-encompassing website spanning travel, attractions, entertainment and sport in the city.

entertainment.ie
Decent guide to all events throughout Ireland, with listings for events, festivals, music, theater and cinema.

heritageireland.ie
Useful in-depth information about historical sites and gardens throughout Ireland.

ireland.com
Tourism Ireland's site carries a wealth of information on the whole of Ireland, with sections on history, culture, events, activities, accommodations and gastronomy, plus plenty of practical tips.

TRAVEL SITES

fodors.com
A complete travel-planning site. You can research prices and weather; book air tickets, cars and rooms; ask questions (and get answers) from fellow travelers; and find links to other sites.

dublinbus.ie
Everything you could possibly need to know about the public bus service, including how to buy the best tickets for your needs. Also information about the DART system and the Luas trams.

USING WIFI

The vast majority of hotels and guesthouses in Dublin have free WiFi for guests. In addition, you'll find that many restaurants and bars will also have a WiFi connection—just ask for their details. Dublin buses, including the airport bus, also have this facility and display the connection details at the front of the bus.

Getting There

ENTRY REQUIREMENTS

Ireland is a member of the European Union (EU). For the most up-to-date passport and visa information visit the Embassy of Ireland Great Britain website (embassyofireland.co.uk) or Embassy of Ireland USA (embassyofireland.org).

CUSTOMS

The limits for non-EU visitors are 200 cigarettes or 50 cigars or 250g of tobacco; 1 liter of spirits (over 22 per cent) or 2 liters of fortified wine, 4 liters of still wine; 50g of perfume. Visitors under 18 are not entitled to the tobacco and alcohol allowances. The guidelines for EU residents (for personal use) are 800 cigarettes, 200 cigars, 1kg of tobacco; 10 liters of spirits (over 22 per cent), 20 liters of aperitifs, 90 liters of wine, of which 60 can be sparkling wine, 110 liters of beer.

AIRPORTS

Dublin Airport is 11km (7 miles) north of the city. It is one of the busiest airports in Europe for international passenger traffic, serving over 180 routes to the UK and continental Europe, US, Canada, North Africa and the Middle East, with some 34 airlines. Aer Lingus is the national carrier.

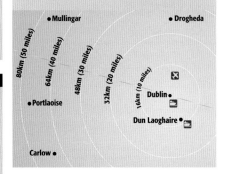

ARRIVING BY AIR

Transportation from Dublin Airport (tel 814 1111, dublinairport.com) is straightforward. Airlink 747 and 757 buses run between the airport and the main city rail and bus stations. The journey takes 20–30 minutes (longer during morning rush hour) and costs €6 one-way, €10 return. Aircoach is a 24-hour luxury coach service serving central Dublin and the main hotels in Ballsbridge/Donnybrook and Leopardstown/Sandyford. The fare ranges from €6 to €9. It also has services to Belfast and Cork. Taxis are metered, and a journey to central Dublin should cost around €30 (but check first). Car rental companies have desks in the arrivals area.

ARRIVING BY BOAT

Ferries from Holyhead and Liverpool sail into the port of Dublin throughout the year. The ferry journey from Holyhead takes around 3 hours 15 minutes on a traditional ferry or 1 hour 50 minutes via the high-speed options. The journey time between Liverpool and Dublin is approximately 8 hours. Taxis and buses

INSURANCE

Check your insurance coverage and buy a supplementary policy if needed. EU nationals receive reduced-cost medical treatment with an EHIC card. Obtain this card before leaving home. Full health and travel insurance is still advised.

operate from the port into the city. From Dublin Port take Alexander Road west, turn left to the 3Arena and follow "city centre" signs.

ARRIVING BY TRAIN

There are two main line train stations in Dublin. Passengers from the north of Ireland arrive at Connolly Station, while trains arriving from the south and west operate in and out of Heuston Station. Buses, taxis and Luas trams are available at Connolly and Heuston stations. Heuston also has a DART stop. Call Irish Rail on 836 6222 or irishrail.ie.

ARRIVING BY CAR

Traffic drives on the left. Congestion in Dublin is notorious, and on-street parking is expensive and limited. There are multistory car parks in the city hub. The one-way traffic systems can be confusing. Avoid rush hours, keep out of bus lanes and use designated parking areas. Penalties for illegal parking are severe. Check whether your hotel or guesthouse has parking for guests. Always lock your car and keep belongings out of sight.

Getting Around

VISITORS WITH DISABILITIES

Access for wheelchair users has improved greatly in Dublin over recent years. Most public buildings and visitor attractions have ramps and lifts. Those with particularly good facilities are the Guinness Storehouse and the Chester Beatty Library. However, it is always wise to phone in advance. Dublin buses have incorporated wheelchair-friendly features into their buses and many of their routes are wheelchair accessible (☎ 703 3024). The Irish Wheelchair Association (☎ 818 6455; iwa.ie) can give advice on accessible accommodations, restaurants and pubs in the city. It can also provide information on wheelchair and car rental.

TAXIS

● Useful numbers:
Taxis
☎ 677 2222; nrc.ie
Blue Cabs
☎ 802 2222;
bluecabs.ie
See local telephone books for others or ask your hotel to call you a cab.

PUBLIC TRANSPORTATION

The bus number and destination (in English and Irish) are displayed on the front. *An Lar* means city center. Buy tickets on the bus (exact change needed) or before boarding from Dublin Bus office or some newsstands; timetables are also available here. Busáras, the main bus terminus, is north of the River Liffey on Amiens Street.

The DART is a light rail service running from Malahide or Howth in the north of the city to Greystones in the south (irishrail.ie). The main city stations are Connolly (north side) and Pearse (south side). Trains run at least every 5 minutes at peak times, otherwise every 15 minutes Mon–Sat 6.30am–11.30pm and less frequently Sun, 9.30am–11pm. Buy tickets at the station.

The Luas is a tram system operating between the suburbs and central Dublin (luas.ie).

Taxis are in short supply, especially at night. Taxi stands are found outside hotels, train and bus stations, and at locations such as St. Stephen's Green and O'Connell Street.

● Dublin Bus (Bus Átha Cliath) operates Mon–Sat 5am–11.30pm, Sun 8am–11.30pm. Check routes (tel 873 4222, dublinbus.ie).
● Nitelink operates Fri–Sat to the suburbs. Buses leave on the hour from D'Olier Street and Westmoreland Street from around midnight to 4.30am; check for individual routes.
● Bus Éireann Expressway operates a nationwide coach service between Dublin and other cities in Ireland (tel 836 6111, buseireann.ie).

TRAVEL PASSES

● The Leap Card, an electronic top-up card for Dublin buses, can be bought for a €5 returnable deposit, topped up with credit. They are not valid for Nitelink, Airlink, ferry services or tours. Fares cost around 20 per cent less than cash tickets.
● You can buy all travel passes from Dublin Bus at 55 Upper O'Connell Street. Selected newsstands sell a limited number of passes.

Essential Facts

ELECTRICITY
● 220V AC. Most hotels have 110V shaver outlets.
● Plugs have three square pins.

EMBASSIES
● Australia: Fitzwilton House, Wilton Terrace, Dublin 2, tel 664 5300, ireland.embassy.gov.au
● Belgium: Shrewsbury Road, Dublin 4, tel 631 5283-86, diplomatie.belgium.be
● Canada: 7–8 Wilton Terrace, Dublin 2, tel 234 4000, canadainternational.gc.ca/ireland-irlande
● France: 66 Fitzwilliam Lane, Dublin 2, tel 277 5000, ambafrance-ie.org
● Germany: 31 Trimleston Avenue, Booterstown, County Dublin, tel 269 3011, dublin.diplo.de
● Italy: 63 Northumberland Road, Dublin 4, tel 660 1744, ambdublino.esteri.it
● Netherlands: 160 Merrion Road, Dublin 4, tel 269 3444, netherlandsembassy.ie
● Spain: 17a Merlyn Park, Dublin 4, tel 269 1640/2597, exteriores.gob.es/embajadas/dublin
● United Kingdom: 29 Merrion Road, Dublin 4, tel 205 3700, britishembassyinireland.fco.gov.uk
● US 42 Elgin Road, Ballsbridge, Dublin 4, tel 668 8777, ie.usembassy.gov

EMERGENCY PHONE NUMBERS
● For Police (*garda*), fire and ambulance call 999 (free of charge).

ETIQUETTE
● Dubliners are very friendly, so do not be perturbed if strangers strike up a conversation.
● Dubliners can be quite laid-back about time-keeping. If you are invited to someone's home for dinner, aim to arrive there about 10 minutes after the arranged time.
● Groups of friends and acquaintances usually buy drinks in rounds and if you join them, you will be expected to participate.

TOURIST INFORMATION
Tourist offices:
⊠ Dublin Airport
⊠ 25 Suffolk Street
⊠ 14 Upper O'Connell Street
⊠ Dun Laoghaire County Hall, Marine Road
All tourist offices are walk-in only. For informaton telephone ☎ 605 7700 (in Ireland) or go to the website: visitdublin.com.

OPENING HOURS
Museums and sights: Most open seven days a week, but some close on Monday, with shorter hours on Sunday. Call for details.
Shops: Open six days a week, some seven days; late-night shopping on Thursday. Supermarkets are open longer hours Wed–Fri. Large suburban shopping malls open Sunday 12–6.
Banks: Mon, Tue, Fri 10–4, Wed 10.30–4, Thu 10–5.

TIPPING

● Tips are not expected in cinemas, fuel stations, or in pubs, unless there is table service.

● Ten per cent is usual for hairdressers and taxi drivers; tip porters, doormen and cloakroom attendants €2. See panel, ▷ 85 for restaurant tipping.

MONEY

The euro has been the official currency of Ireland since 2002. Bank notes are in denominations of 5, 10, 20, 50, 100, 200 and 500 euros, and coins in denominations of 5, 10, 20 and 50 cents and 1 and 2 euros (1 and 2 cent coins are being phased out).

LGBT TRAVELERS

● GCN (Gay Community News) is a free monthly magazine and is available in bars, clubs and bookshops (theoutmost.com) throughout the city.

● LGBT events in Dublin include the International Dublin Gay Theater Festival (May), Pride (late June) and the Lesbian and Gay Film Festival (late July/August).

● For information and advice, contact: Gay Switchboard Dublin (tel 872 1055, gayswitchboard.ie, open Mon–Fri 6.30pm–9pm, Sat 2–6, Sun 4–6); Outhouse LGBT (105 Capel Street, tel 873 4999, outhouse.ie).

MEDICINES AND MEDICAL TREATMENT

● Ambulance: tel 999 or 112.

● Hospital with 24-hour emergency service: St. James's Hospital (James's Street, Dublin 8; tel 410 3000).

● Dental: emergency treatment (daytimes only): Dublin Dental University Hospital (Lincoln Place; tel 612 7391).

● Minor ailments can usually be treated at pharmacies, but only a limited range of medication can be dispensed without a prescription.

● Pharmacies in Dublin that are open late: Hickey's Pharmacy (55 Lower O'Connell Street, tel 873 0427), City Pharmacy (14 Dame Street, 670 4523).

MONEY MATTERS

● Banks may offer better exchange rates than shops, hotels and bureaux de change.

● The bank at Dublin airport has longer opening hours but charges above-average commission.

● Credit and debit cards can be used in most hotels, shops and restaurants and to withdraw cash from ATMs.

● Currency cards, which you top-up online, can be used to withdraw cash or used as a debit card, and generally attract little or no commission.

NEWSPAPERS AND MAGAZINES

● The daily broadsheets, the *Irish Times* and the *Irish Independent*, are printed in Dublin. The local *Evening Herald* is on sale Mon–Fri at midday. The major UK tabloids also produce separate Irish editions.

● International magazines and newspapers are sold in major bookstores including Eason (40–42 Lower O'Connell Street).

● For events and entertainment listings, check out the free *In Dublin* and *Totally Dublin* magazines.

● *Hot Press* is Ireland's music magazine and *Image* is Ireland's popular women's magazine. UK magazines are widely available.

ORGANIZED TOURS

● Dublin Bus Tour is a hop-on, hop-off city sightseeing tour. Buy tickets on board the buses or at Dublin Tourism in Suffolk Street before you begin your tour.

● The Dublin Literary Pub Crawl is a walking tour that visits pubs frequented by historic literary giants. Guides add to the atmosphere by giving readings from famous Irish tomes. The tour starts from the Duke pub, Duke Street (tel 670 5602; runs Apr–Oct nightly 7.30pm; Nov–Mar Thu–Sun 7.30pm).

● The Musical Pub Crawl starts from the Oliver St. John Gogarty pub (tel 475 3313; runs Apr–Oct nightly 7.30pm; Nov–Mar Thu–Sat 7.30pm).

● Take a sightseeing boat cruise with Dublin Discovered and learn about life in Dublin from the Vikings to the latest redevelopment (tel 473 0000; sailings depart from Batchelor's Walk, daily from 11.30am, Mar–Nov).

POST OFFICES

● The main post office, GPO, in O'Connell Street (tel 705 8833) is open Mon–Sat 8.30–6. Other post offices are generally open Mon–Fri 9–5.30, and certain city branches also open on Saturday. Some suburban offices may close at lunchtime.

NATIONAL HOLIDAYS

● 1 January; 17 March; Easter Monday; first Monday in May, June and August; last Monday in October; 25 and 26 December.

● Many businesses close on Good Friday.

TOILETS

● Dublin is not noted for its public toilets: use the facilities at a pub, shopping mall or large store.

● Signs may be in Irish: *mná*: women, *fir*: men.

LOST PROPERTY

Report loss or theft of a passport to the police immediately. Your embassy or consulate can provide further assistance.

Airport ☎ 814 5555
Ferry port ☎ 607 5519
Train ☎ 703 3299 (Heuston), 703 2358 (Connolly)
Dublin Bus ☎ 703 1321
Bus Éireann ☎ 836 6111

STUDENTS

● Dublin is very student-friendly.
● An International Student Identity Card (ISIC) secures discounts in many cinemas, theaters, shops, restaurants and attractions.
● Discounts may be available on travel cards for the bus and DART.

● Stamps are sold at post offices, some news-stands, hotels and shops. Stamps are also available from coin-operated machines.
● Postboxes are green.

SENSIBLE PRECAUTIONS

● Dublin is generally safe but be cautious and keep valuables out of sight.
● Don't leave handbags on the backs of chairs.
● Make a separate note of all passport, ticket and credit card numbers.
● Avoid Phoenix Park at night.
● After dark, women should sit downstairs on buses, or in a busy car on trains. Take a taxi rather than a late-night bus out to the suburbs.

TELEPHONES

● Public telephones use coins or phone cards (sold in post offices and newsagents).
● For the operator, dial 10; for directory enquiries dial 11850, 11890 or 11811.
● Calls from hotels are expensive. Look for public phones on streets, in pubs and shopping malls. Make the most of free WiFi in hotels, restaurants, etc, to make international calls from your smartphone with Whatsapp or Viber.
● If you are in Dublin for a longer stay, it could be worthwhile buying a local SIM card for your mobile phone if it is unlocked.
● When calling Ireland from the UK dial 00 353. The code for Dublin is 01 (omit the zero when calling from abroad).
● To call the UK from Dublin, dial 00 44.
● When calling from the US dial 011 353. The code for Dublin is 01 (omit the zero when calling from abroad).
● To call the US from Dublin, dial 00 1.

TV AND RADIO

● Radio Telefis Éireann (RTÉ) is the state broad-casting authority. It has four FM radio stations and five digital radio stations. Its television stations are RTÉ 1, RTÉ 2 and RTÉ News Now.
● TG4 is the National Irish Language station. TV3 Ireland is independent.

Language

Irish is the official first language of the Republic of Ireland with English, although English is the spoken language in Dublin. It is uncommon to hear Irish spoken in Dublin, but the language is enjoying a revival and is fashionable among a younger set proud of their cultural traditions. It is an important symbol of national identity. You will come across Irish on sign-posts, buses, trains and official documents, and the news (*an nuacht*) is broadcast *as gaeilge* on television and radio. Telefis Na Gaeilge's *TG4* is a dedicated Irish-language channel with English subtitles. The areas known as the Gaeltacht are pockets of the country where Irish is the main tongue and you will find maps and signposts using only the Gaelic. These areas are mainly on the western side of Ireland. The Irish language is difficult for the beginner to grasp, with words often pronounced quite differently to the way they are written. To complicate things further, there are different Irish dialects and spellings in different regions.

SOME IRISH WORDS TO LOOK OUT FOR

An Lar	City center	*Leitris*	Toilet
Baile Átha Cliath	Dublin	*Mná*	Ladies
Céilí	Dance	*Fir*	Gents
Craic	Good time	*Le do thoil*	Please
Dia dhuit	Hello	*Níl/ní hea*	No
Dúnta	Closed	*Oifig an phoist*	Post Office
Fáilte	Welcome	*Oscailte*	Open
Gardaí	Police	*Slán*	Goodbye
Go raibh maith aguth	Thank you	*Sláinte*	Cheers
		Tá/sea	Yes

PLACE NAMES AND THEIR IRISH ROOT

IRISH ROOT	MEANING	IRISH PLACE NAMES
ar, ard	height	Ardmore, Ardgroom
áth, atha	ford	Athlone, Athy
bal, baile, ballya	town	Ballyhack
beg, beag	small	Beaghmore Stone Circles, Lough Beg
cashel	castle	Rock of Cashel
drom, drum	a ridge	Drombeg Stone Circle, Drumsna
dun, dún	a fort	Dundalk, Dún Laoghaire
innis, ennis	island	Enniskerry, Enniscorthy
kil, kill, cil	a church	Killarney, Glencolumbkille
knock, cnoc	a hill	Knocknarea Mountain, Knockferry
lis, liss, lios	a ring fort	Listowel, Lisdoonvarna
mor, mór	big or great	Aranmore, Lismore
rath	a ring fort	Rathfarnham, Rathdrum
slieve	a mountain	Slieve Bloom, Slieve League

Timeline

BEFORE AD1000

The Celts landed in Ireland in the 4th century BC and their influence remains even today. Their religious rites included complex burial services. Archeological excavations have produced some magnificent gold pieces and jewelry, some of which can be seen in the National Museum (▷ 68).

According to legend, St. Patrick converted many of Dublin's inhabitants to Christianity in the fifth century AD. In AD841 Vikings established a trading station, probably near present-day Kilmainham. The Vikings later moved downstream, to the area around Dublin Castle, in the 10th century.

1014 High King Brian Boru defeats the Dublin Vikings.

1172 After Norman barons invade Ireland from Wales, King Henry II gives Dublin to the men of Bristol.

1348–51 The Black Death claims one third of Dublin's inhabitants.

1592 Queen Elizabeth I grants a charter for the founding of Trinity College.

1700s Dublin's population expands from 40,000 to 172,000.

1713 Jonathan Swift is appointed Dean of St. Patrick's Cathedral.

1714 Start of the Georgian era, Dublin's great period of classical architecture.

1745 The building of Leinster House (now home of the Irish Parliament) leads to new housing south of the river.

1759 The Guinness Brewery is founded.

1782 The Irish Parliament secures legislative independence from Britain.

1800 The Act of Union is passed and the Irish Parliament abolishes itself.

1845 The start of Ireland's Great Famine.

1916 The Easter Rising.

1919 First session of Dáil Éireann (the Irish Parliament) in Mansion House.

1922 Civil War declared. After 718 years in residence, British forces evacuate Dublin Castle.

1963 Visit by President John F. Kennedy.

1979 The Pope says mass in Phoenix Park to more than 1.3 million people.

1990 Mary Robinson is elected president—Ireland's first female president.

1997 Divorce becomes legal under certain circumstances.

1998 The Good Friday Agreement sees a ceasefire in Northern Ireland.

2001 IRA is decommissioned in December.

2011 Queen Elizabeth II is the first British monarch to visit Ireland since its independence.

2013 Legislation is passed allowing abortion in certain circumstances.

2015 A referendum results in Ireland legalizing same-sex marriage.

2017 Ireland hosts the Women's Rugby World Cup.

EASTER RISING

With the founding of the Gaelic League in 1893 and the Abbey Theatre in 1904, the movement for independence gathered momentum in Ireland. Republicans capitalized on England's preoccupation with World War I to stage a rising in 1916 and declare an independent Republic in Dublin's General Post Office. It was doomed to failure but the execution of several of the insurrection's leaders made rebels out of many Irish royalists, leading five years later to the creation of an Irish Free State. The Anglo-Irish Treaty was signed in 1921, followed by a Civil War in 1922, lasting 22 months. In 1936 the Free State became known as Eire under a new Constitution. The Republic finally became a reality in 1949.

From far left: An early city map; helmets in St. Patrick's Cathedral; Great Courtyard of Dublin Castle; Queen Victoria visits Dublin (1900)

Index

CityPack Dublin

Published by AA Publishing, a trading name of AA Media Limited, whose registered office is Fanum House, Basing View, Basingstoke, Hampshire RG21 4EA. Registered number 06112600.

© AA Media Limited 2018
First published 1999
Revised and updated 2015
New edition 2018. Reprinted July 2018.

Written by Dr. Peter Harbison and Melanie Morris
Additional writing Hilary Weston and Jackie Staddon
Updated by Emma Levine
Series editor Clare Ashton
Design work Liz Baldin
Image retouching and repro Ian Little

Colour separation by AA Digital Department
Printed and bound by Leo Paper Products, China

A CIP catalogue record for this book is available from the British Library.

ISBN 978-0-7495-7933-3

A05650

Maps in this title based on Ordnance Survey Ireland.
Permit No. 9098
© Ordnance Survey Ireland and Government of Ireland
Includes data from openstreetmap.org © OpenStreetMap contributors
Transport map © Communicarta Ltd, UK

The Automobile Association would like to thank the following photographers, companies and picture libraries for their assistance in the preparation of this book.

2–4t AA/S Day; 4l AA/S Whitehorne; 5t AA/S Day; 5c AA/S Whitehorne; 6t AA/S Day; 6cl AA/C Coe; 6c AA/Slidefile; 6cr AA/M Short; 6bl Ireland's Content Pool; 6bc AA/S Whitehorne; 6br AA/S McBride; 7t AA/S Day; 7cl AA/L Blake; 7cr AA/S Day; 7bl AA/S Day; 7br Ireland's Content Pool/Tony Pleavin; 8t AA/S Day; 9t AA/S Day; 10t AA/S Day; 10ctr AA/S Whitehorne; 10cr AA/S Day; 10cbr Ireland's Content Pool/Tourism Ireland; 11t AA/S Day; 11ctl Ireland's Content Pool/Jonathon Hessian; 11cl–11cbl Ireland's Content Pool; 12 AA/S Day; 13t AA/S Day; 13ctl AA/Slidefile; 13cl Ireland's Content Pool/Rob Durston Photography; 13cbl AA/Slidefile; 13bl Ireland's Content Pool/Tony Pleavin; 14t AA/S Day; 14ctr AA/S McBride; 14cr AA/S Day; 14cbr Ireland's Content Pool/Tourism Ireland; 14br AA/S Whitehorne; 15 AA/S Day; 16t AA/S Day; 16tr AA/S Whitehorne; 16cr Photodisc; 16br AA/D Henley; 17t AA/S Day; 17tl AA/M Short; 17ctl Buswell's Hotel, Dublin; 17c Photodisc; 17cbl Ireland's Content Pool/DRTA; 17bl Dublin Zoo; 18t AA/S Day; 18tr AA/S Day; 18ctr Ireland's Content Pool/Tourism Ireland; 18cbr AA/Slidefile; 18br Ireland's Content Pool; 19t Courtesy of Guiness Storehouse; 19ct–19cb AA/S Day; 19b AA/S Whitehorne; 20/21 AA/S Day; 24l AA/S Whitehorne; 24c AA/S Day; 24r AA/Slidefile; 25l AA/S Day; 25r–26 Ireland's Content Pool/Rob Durston Photographer; 27tl AA/S Day; 27tr AA/S Day; 27cl Ireland's Content Pool/Rob Durston Photographer; 27cr AA/S Day; 28, 29t, 29cl, 29cr Dublinia Ltd; 30t Ireland's Content Pool/Rob Durston Photographer; 30c–30/31 Courtesy of Guinness Storehouse; 32l AA/S Whitehorne; 32c AA/S Day; 32r AA/S Day; 33l Ireland's Content Pool/Rob Durston Photographer; 33r Ireland's Content Pool/davisonphoto.com; 34l AA/S Day; 34r AA/C Coe; 35t AA/Slidefile; 35bl AA/S Day; 35br AA/S Whitehorne; 36 AA/S Whitehorne; 37 AA/S Whitehorne; 38 AA/S Whitehorne; 39 AA/Slidefile; 40t AA/Slidefile; 41t AA/Slidefile; 41c Ireland's Content Pool/Rob Durston Photographer; 42t Ireland's Content Pool/Rob Durston Photography; 43t Ireland's Content Pool/Rob Durston Photography; 44t Rob Durston Photography; 45 Hon Lau - Dublin/ Alamy Stock Photo; 48 National Museum of Decorative Arts; 49l Courtesy of Hugh Lane Gallery; 49r Ireland's Content Pool; 50l AA/S Day; 50c Ireland's Content Pool/DRTA; 50r AA/M Short; 51 Ireland's Content Pool/Epic Ireland Property; 52l Ireland's Content Pool; 52r Ireland's Content Pool; 53l Killian Broderick/James Joyce Centre; 53c AA/S Day; 53r Ireland's Content Pool/Brian Morrison; 54/5, 55t, 55c Jameson Distillery Bow Street; 56t AA/Slidefile; 56bl AA/Slidefile; 56br AA/Slidefile; 57t AA/Slidefile; 58t AA/S Whitehorne; 59t Ireland's Content Pool/Clara Hooper; 60t DigitalVision; 61t DigitalVision; 61c AA/S McBride; 62t AA/S McBride; 63 Ireland's Content Pool/Brian Morrison; 66l, 66r Little Museum of Dublin; 67l, 67r Ireland's Content Pool; 68 Ireland's Content Pool/Rob Durston Photography; 68/9 AA/S Day; 70tl Ireland's Content Pool/Tony Pearson; 70cl Ireland's Content Pool/Niamh Fahy; 71 Ireland's Content Pool/Niamh Fahy; 72t Ireland's Content Pool/Brian Morrison; 72c Ireland's Content Pool/Brian Morrison; 72/3 AA/S McBride; 74t AA/Slidefile; 74b Ireland's Content Pool/Jonathon Hessian; 75t AA/Slidefile; 75b Ireland's Content Pool/Matthew Thompson; 76t AA/Slidefile; 76bl Ireland's Content Pool; 76br Viking Splash; 77 AA/S Whitehorne; 78–81t Ireland's Content Pool/Tourism Ireland; 82t Ireland's Content Pool/Rob Durston Photography; 83t Ireland's Content Pool/Rob Durston Photography; 84t Ireland's Content Pool/Rob Durston Photography; 85c AA/S Day; 85t AA/S Day; 86t AA/S Day; 87t AA/S Day; 88t AA/S Day; 89 AA/C Jones; 92l Patrick Bolger/ Dublin Zoo; 92r Patrick Bolger/Dublin Zoo; 93 GAA Museum; 94l Ireland's Content Pool/ Peter Moloney; 94r Ireland's Content Pool/Peter Moloney; 96l AA/S Whitehorne; 96tr AA/S Whitehorne; 97t AA/Slidefile; 97bl AA/S Whitehorne; 98t AA/Slidefile; 98b AA/S Whitehorne; 99 Dublin Zoo; 100t AA/M Short; 100cl AA/M Short; 100cr AA/M Short; 100br AA/C Jones; 101t AA/M Short; 101bl AA/S Whitehorne; 102t AA/C Jones; 102bl AA/C Jones; 102br AA/C Jones; 103t AA/C Jones; 103bl AA/Slidefile; 103bc AA/M Short; 103br AA/M Short; 104t AA/M Short; 104c AA/Slidefile; 105t AA/Slidefile; 106t ImageState; 107 AA/C Sawyer; 108t AA/C Sawyer; 108ctr AA/W Vosey; 108cr AA/C Sawyer; 108cbr Buswell's Hotel, Dublin; 108br AA/S McBride; 109t AA/C Sawyer; 110t AA/C Sawyer; 111t AA/C Sawyer; 112t AA/C Sawyer; 113 AA/K Blackwell; 114 Ireland's Content Pool; 115 Ireland's Content Pool; 116 Ireland's Content Pool; 117t Ireland's Content Pool; 117c AA/C Jones; 117b AA/M Short; 118t Ireland's Content Pool; 119b Ireland's Content Pool; 120t–124t Ireland's Content Pool; 124bl AA/Slidefile; 124bc AA/S Day; 124/125 AA/Slidefile; 125t Ireland's Content Pool; 125br AA.

Every effort has been made to trace the copyright holders, and we apologise in advance for any accidental errors. We would be happy to apply the corrections in the following edition of this publication.

Titles in the Series